SEA
Tel-Aviv
Jaffa
PETAH TIVAH
MIKVEH ISRAEL
RISHON LEZION
Ben Shemen
Lod
Rehovot
Ramallah
Jericho
JORDAN
Hulda
Gederah
Kiryat Anavim
Har-Tov
Jerusalem
Bethlehem
Ashkelon
Hebron
Sderot Rothschild
Gaza
Ein-Gedi
DEAD SEA
TRANSJ
Beersheba
NEGEV
El Arish
EGYPT
palacios

Coming Home to Zion

Other books by Abraham Shulman

THE OLD COUNTRY
THE NEW COUNTRY

Shepherds in Valley of Jezreel

COMING HOME to ZION

A Pictorial History of Pre-Israel Palestine

Abraham Shulman

Doubleday & Company, Inc.
Garden City, New York
1979

The author and publisher express their appreciation to the WORKERS' BOOK-GUILD (HASHOMER HATZAIR) LTD, *Tel Aviv, Israel, for the poem, "Dress Me, Mother" by Avraham Shlonsky.*

The author and publisher express their appreciation to the following for permission to include photos from their collections:

ARCHIVES AND MUSEUM OF THE JEWISH LABOUR MOVEMENT: *Tel Aviv, Israel*
THE CENTRAL ZIONIST ARCHIVES: *Jerusalem, Israel*
HAGANA MUSEUM: *Tel Aviv, Israel*
THE JEWISH DAILY FORWARD: *New York, New York*
MUSEUM OF THE HISTORY OF TEL AVIV-YAFO: *Tel Aviv, Israel*
MUSEUM OF ISRAEL'S DEFENSE FORCES: *Tel Aviv, Israel*
THEATER MUSEUM: *Tel Aviv, Israel*
THE ZIONIST ARCHIVES AND LIBRARY: *New York, New York*

Library of Congress Cataloging in Publication Data

Shulman, Abraham.
Coming home to Zion.

1. Zionism—History. 2. Jews in Palestine—History. 3. Palestine—Emigration and immigration.
I. Title.
DS149.S49793 956.94'001
ISBN: 0-385-14256-0
Library of Congress Catalog Card Number 78-14187

Designed by Betsy Beach

Printed in the United States of America
FIRST EDITION

To my children,
Chava and David

Acknowledgments

I'd like to thank all those who were instrumental in helping me research this book. The following people were particularly co-operative in lending their assistance: Dr. Michael Hayman and Mrs. Adina Haran of The Central Zionist Archives in Jerusalem, Dr. Anina Kaplan of the Museum of the History of Tel Aviv-Yafo, Mrs. Musia Lipman of the Archives and Museum of the Jewish Labour Movement in Tel Aviv, Mr. Joseph Kopiloff of the Museum of Israel's Defense Forces, Mr. Yehuda Gabai of the Theater Museum in Tel Aviv, Mr. M. Petrushka, Association President, and Mr. Harry Ostroff, General Manager, of *The Jewish Daily Forward,* and Mrs. Sylvia Landess of The Zionist Archives and Library in New York.

A. Shulman

Contents

Introduction

ISRAEL is a Jewish state that has come into existence as the result of the longing, the faith, and the determination of an ancient people. The book of Abraham Shulman, *Coming Home to Zion,* is an attempt to demonstrate—with the help of rare and exquisite photographs—how this state of longing has been transformed into reality.

It is a pictorial history of the dream that has lived in the Jewish mind since the destruction of the Temple; of how this dream has developed from a mystical, religious, and liturgical beginning until it has attained the dimension of a political movement; and finally, how this movement has consequently taken shape in human acts that have become the foundations of the Jewish state.

The book contains marvelous, rarely or never before published photos depicting the very early days, when the name Zionism hadn't yet been formulated; when the longing had only begun to take root in the villages, townships, and towns mostly of eastern Europe; when the dream had been carried over to the redeemed land by the earliest pioneers and settlers.

The book contains a richness of photos diligently and with devotion collected by the author from many sources. They illustrate how the idea of "being a nation like all nations" had begun to spread at the turn of the century through the Jewish communities of Europe; how the first individuals had ventured to Palestine in order to rehabilitate the land, living in a state of self-abnegation and austerity; how this trickle of colonization gradually had transformed into a political orientation formulated at the First Zionist Congress, in Basel, as "the objective of Zionism is to establish for the Jewish people a publicly and legally assured home in Palestine"; and at last, how the dead, devastated, and neglected land has slowly become the flourishing Israel.

There are many books dealing with that period. This is the first attempt to tell this story by way of revealing photos. Abraham Shulman's *Coming Home to Zion* can serve as an impressive corollary to books dealing with that dramatic phase of Jewish history; it can also serve as an independent history book of the great prologue to the Jewish state told by so many moving, often pathetic, and artistically inspired photos showing how the Promised Land was becoming the Land of Promise.

—*Golda Meir*

Coming Home to Zion

I

By the Rivers of Babylon

TRADITIONAL Jewish weddings have one curious custom: The bridegroom, after putting the ring on his bride's finger and pronouncing the nine words of betrothal, is handed a glass which he promptly breaks underfoot. This custom puzzles many; only a few know that the breaking of the glass is one of the many symbols that express the Jewish yearning for their lost nationhood.

The sound of the broken glass is a reminder of the destruction of the Temple. It is one of the many manifestations of the longing for national revival which never ceased to attend the Jewish people during the two thousand years of their exile.

Not for one day of the year is a Jew allowed to forget that national catastrophe. He must pray three times a day with his face to the east, in the direction of Jerusalem. On the anniversary of the destruction of the Temple, on the ninth day of Av, he must spend the whole day in *shul* sitting on the floor or on an overturned bench, in his stockinged feet, like a mourner at the death of a family member, and chanting the *Psalm of Lamentation.* The same Psalm, "By the rivers of Babylon," is used in the blessing asked three times daily after meals. At the act of circumcision, the ceremony at which the eight-year-old boy enters into the covenant with God, mention is made of the old divine promise given to Abraham, the first Jew, about the land of Canaan. Pious Jews, before putting on any new clothes, will soil them slightly as a symbol of unceasing national grief. When renovating a house, at least one brick must be left unpainted for the same reason. Such reminders accompany a Jew even into his grave. In the shtetls of eastern Europe it was customary to put a bag of earth from the Holy Land under the head of the corpse, so that he might rest on sacred soil.

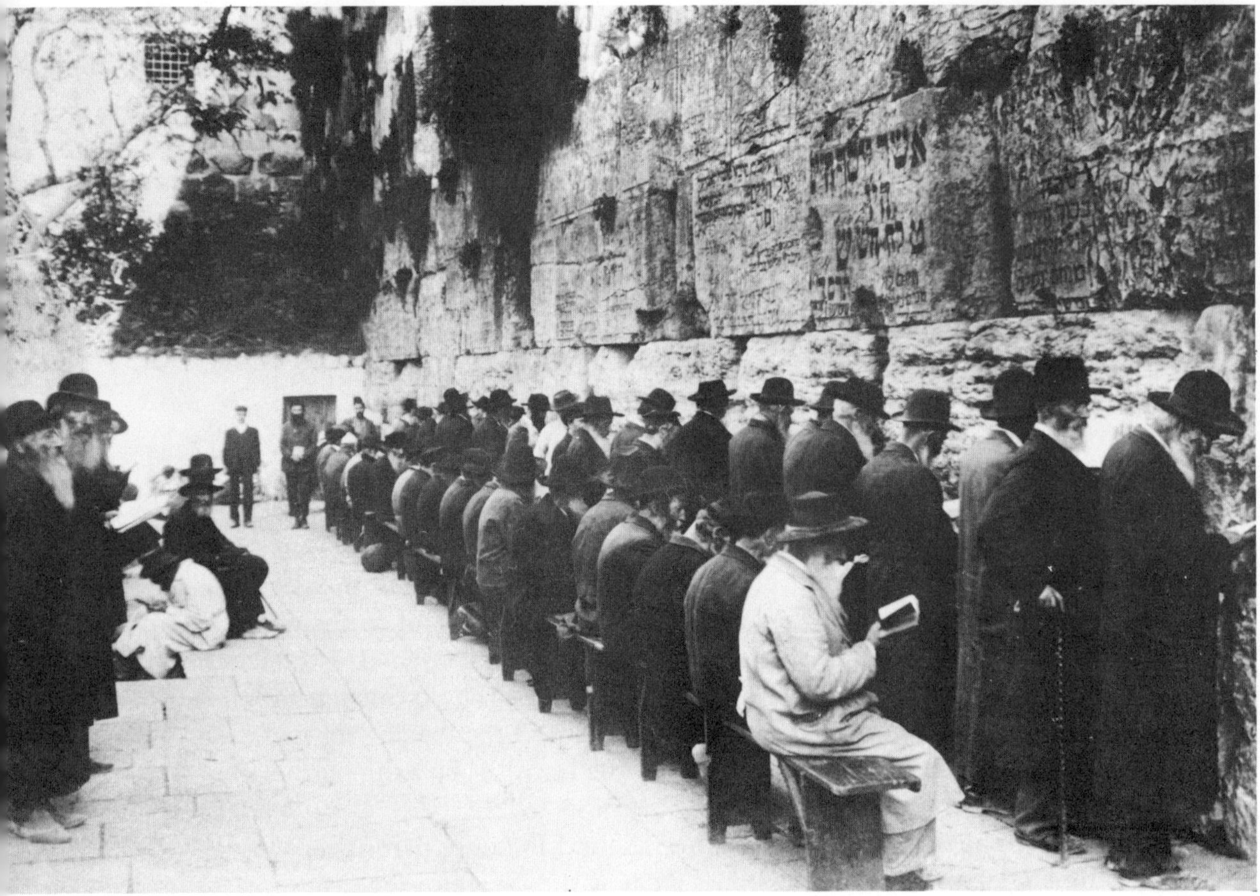

The Central Zionist Archives, Jerusalem, Israel

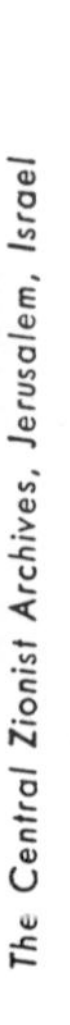

The Wailing Wall, 1912

And so, throughout the long history of dispersion, the Jew, often subject to the worst forms of persecution, would look beyond the walls of the ghetto and see the walls of Jerusalem. He believed that the pains and tribulations were nothing but a transitory stage: the trumpet of the Messiah could sound at any minute; the living and the dead could be brought from the four corners of the earth and gathered together in the reborn homeland.

This perpetual state of waiting for redemption has helped keep the spirit alive under trying, even murderous conditions. It was easier to live in the glories of the past and in waiting for a similar glorious future.

The Central Zionist Archives, Jerusalem, Israel

Gate of Damascus, 1912

Nonetheless, the ever-repeated wish "Next year in Jerusalem" never, in the course of all these hundreds of years, gave birth to a movement that would call upon the Jews actually to rise up and return to the lost land.

Pious Jews would never have considered it; such a thought would be blasphemous, for it would mean taking upon themselves a role that could be performed only by God. Others wouldn't consider it for different reasons: In the first place, the various rulers of the countries they lived in would not allow the exiled Jews to return to the land from which they had once been banished. But even if they did return, Palestine had become a devastated and backward country, neglected or often deliberately destroyed by its many masters. It was a poor and primitive land, ridden with disease and crime. To make the arduous journey from

The Central Zionist Archives, Jerusalem, Israel

Old shul *in Safed*

The Central Zionist Archives, Jerusalem, Israel

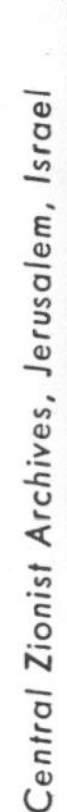

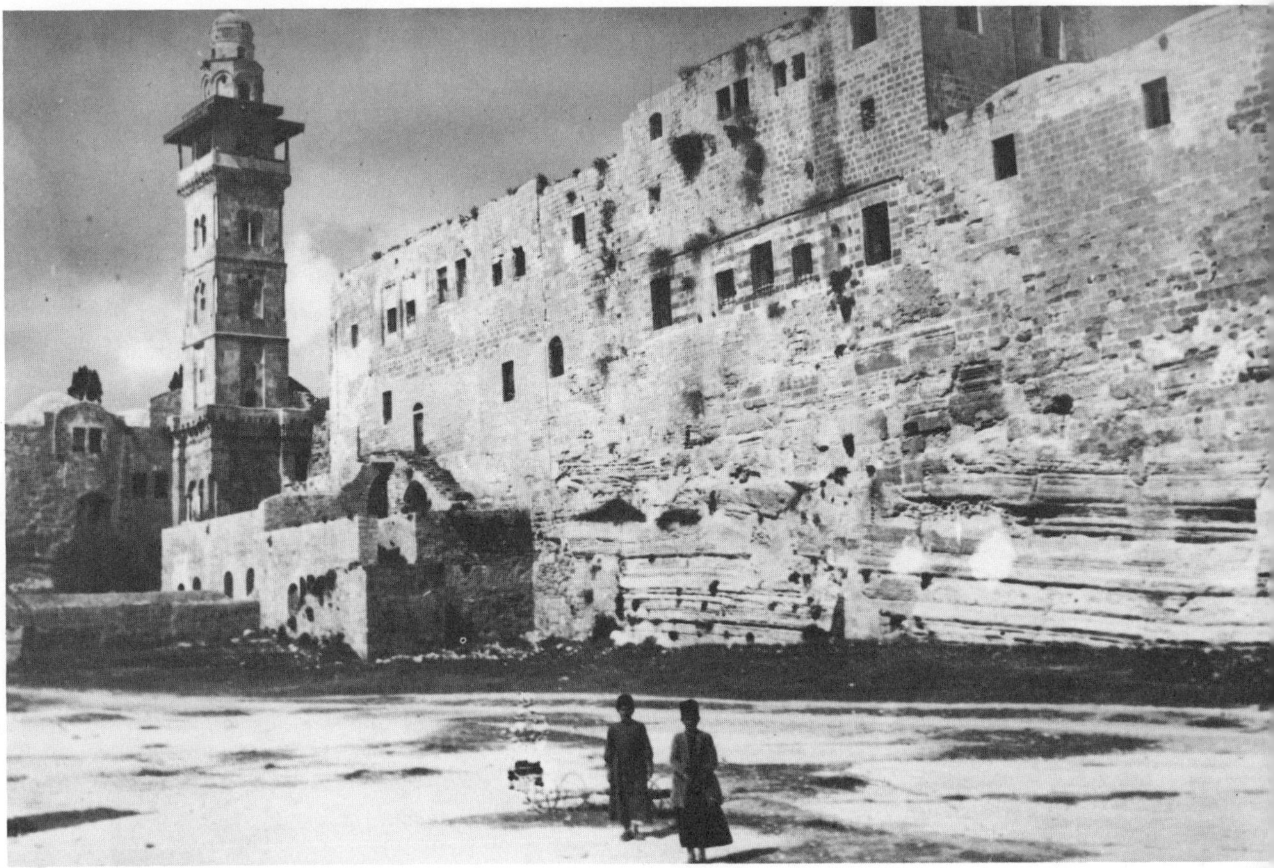

The temple courtyard, 1915

the places of dispersion to Palestine would mean running away from the hardship and peril of one place to another where the hardships and the dangers would not be less.

Only from time to time would a Jew, and then usually an elderly one, risk the hardships of the journey to settle in one of the four holy cities: Jerusalem, Safed, Hebron, and Tiberias. He would be religiously motivated: he would go there to be able to pray on the holy sites, to live near the Gate of Compassion, through which the Messiah would come riding on a white donkey; but above all, when his time came to be "gathered into the ancestors," to be buried in hallowed ground.

The number of such Jews remained small: by 1839 their total, including those who studied in the *yeshivot*, didn't exceed thirteen thousand. Most of them lived in extreme poverty, on charity collected from the towns and villages of eastern Europe by roaming emissaries. This constant though small community of Jews would have continued to live forever in the same state of stagnation, had it not been for an event that occurred in the year 1882. In that year, more precisely on the eleventh day of August, a group of young Jews from the Russian city of Kharkov set out for Palestine with a new purpose: they went there not to die but to live; they went there determined to transform into reality a dream that was two thousand years old but that until then had lived only in symbols: broken glasses, unpainted bricks, and the forever-repeated abstract wish of "Next year in Jerusalem."

The fourteen young Jews from Kharkov, thirteen boys and one girl,* didn't simply go to Palestine, but they returned to Zion.

* The first group of Bilu (see Chapter III) comprised thirteen people. However, one of the Bilu had come earlier. He, Yakov Shertok, was there when the other thirteen arrived; he became the father of the late minister Moshe Sharett.

II

Western European Origins of a Miracle

The movement to return to Zion, ironically, began in Europe in the nineteenth century. The word "ironically" applies in this case because the movement of Zionism, which in reality meant escape from the countries of dispersion, was born in a century when it had seemed that the reason for escape had at last vanished. The movement of Enlightenment started in the eighteenth century, first appearing in Germany and spreading to all corners of Europe. The movement proclaimed that the hitherto isolated Jew could be brought into final rapprochement with his non-Jewish neighbors. The choice, according to the preachers of the Enlightenment, lay in the hands of the Jew. All he had to do was to purge his Jewish way of life of its "medieval obscurantism" and westernize his religion and customs. The barriers between Jew and gentile would then disappear and all anti-Jewish prejudice melt like snow.

This optimism emanated from Germany and reached the heartland of the Jews in Russia; it was further strengthened by the French Revolution, which adopted the unprecedented Declaration of the Rights of Man, announcing that all men are created equal. For the first time in their history of exile, the Jews were included in the trinity of Liberty, Equality, and even Fraternity.

Later, the victorious Napoleonic armies carried this spirit of humanism to other countries of Europe; wherever the soldiers with their tricolor ribbons appeared, ghetto walls crumbled, and old biases and hostilities were erased. Even later, when the defeat of the Little Corporal caused the re-emergence of reactionary regimes, the revolutions of 1848, which followed, put the finishing touch on the work begun by the sans-culottes of Paris. The revolutions of 1848 have been called the

Spring of Nations. For the Jews of western and central Europe, more than for anybody else, this was indeed a time redolent of spring.

Many Jews were so enthused with the prospect of becoming like the *goyim,* that they were ready to go one step further and become complete *goyim.* They believed that the ceremony of baptism would give them what one convert, Heinrich Heine, had satirically named "the entrance key to civilization." But the supporters of Enlightenment and the holders of this entrance key were treading on quicksand.

In 1894 the trial of a French Jewish army officer, Alfred Dreyfus, accused of treason, aroused a furious wave of anti-Semitism, which swept over France. It came so unexpectedly and with such force that the French Jews, still under the spell of the Enlightenment, were hardly able to rally before it was followed by a new kind of anti-Semitism, launched by a French "scholar," Gobineau, which spread over western Europe, finding particularly fertile ground in Germany. This anti-Semitism was based on "scientific" theories of race that not only shattered the optimism of the enlightened assimilationists but closed the door to the whole non-Jewish society even to the converts, those holders of the illusionary "keys."

It was an agonizing blow to all those who believed in the human impact of Emancipation—the term referring to the prior, liberal government policy toward Jews. Their frustration was so profound that from the depth of their milieu arose words of bitter disappointment. One of them, the Hegelian philosopher Moses Hess, a former collaborator of Marx and Engels, found himself betrayed by both his hopes in Emancipation and by the promises of socialism. He came to the conclusion that the situation of the Jews was not unlike that of the proletariat. Along the lines of the Communist Manifesto, he substituted for "class" in "class struggle," the words "oppressed nationality." Only in a home of his own would the Jew function as a free man and a liberated human being. Moses Hess, who had formerly, along with Marx, believed that the liberation of the toiling masses would mean the redemption of the whole world, now shifted his view from the liberation of the masses to the national liberation of Jews. The revival of the Jewish state, he concluded, would mark the beginning of a spiritual revival of humanity. It would be the Messianic sign of the liberation of all oppressed individuals and nations.

The Central Zionist Archives, Jerusalem, Israel

Moses Hess (1811–75)

His book *Rome and Jerusalem,* published in 1862, was the first appeal for the revival of the Jewish homeland without recourse to the emotional mystique. For a long time, this book went unnoticed. Its importance became known much later, when another disillusioned Jewish assimilationist came out with a public plea that eventually changed the course of Jewish history. His name was Theodor Herzl.

The nineteenth century was the age of lofty and passionate words, and this is how Herzl put into words the anxiety caused by the general disappointment:

> *We have sincerely tried everywhere to merge with the national communities in which we live, seeking only to preserve the faith of our fathers. It is not permitted to us. In vain are we loyal patriots, sometimes superloyal; in vain do we make the same sacrifices of life and property as our fellow citizens; in vain do we strive to enhance the fame of our native land in arts and sciences, or her wealth by trade and commerce. In our native land where we have lived for centuries we are still decried as aliens, often by men whose ancestors had not yet come at a time when Jewish sighs had long been heard in the country. The government decides who the alien is. . . . In the world as it is now and will probably remain for an indefinite period, might takes precedence over right. It is without avail, therefore, for us to be loyal patriots, as were the Huguenots, who were forced to emigrate. If we were left in peace. . . . But I think we shall not be left in peace.*

The last sentence from this passage of his book *Judenstaat,* published in 1896, has a somber and prophetic sound.

It is strange that this man, born into an assimilated Jewish family in Budapest, without a trace of Jewish tradition and very little awareness, if not complete unawareness, of the Messianic symbols of the eastern European Jews, had nevertheless, only a few years after he discovered the road to Zion, been able to enter their metaphysical universe and become their long-awaited Messiah.

His small brochure *Judenstaat* had a great impact both on Jews and non-Jews, and no less impact was made by his personality and behavior. Herzl was a journalist of European renown and also a playwright; his fascination with the stage no doubt enhanced his role as a national leader. The First Zionest Congress, arranged under his direction, had the splendor of a theatrical gala performance. He demanded of all the delegates, even those who came from obscure little places in the Russian Pale of Settlement, to wear top hats, frock coats, and white ties for the ceremony of the "nation's rebirth."

First Zionist Congress, in Basel, Switzerland, 1897

The Central Zionist Archives, Jerusalem, Israel

The Central Zionist Archives, Jerusalem, Israel

Young Theodor Herzl and his sister, Pauline

Herzl (first from the right) as member of student aliyah *organization*

The Central Zionist Archives, Jerusalem, Israel

Herzl en route to Palestine

The Central Zionist Archives, Jerusalem, Israel

Herzl leaving synagogue, 1903

His later audiences with the Turkish sultan, the German emperor, the Italian king, and with leaders of the British Government had all the elements of grandiose theater. He lent glitter and dignity to the political movement that he created, as one of the delegates to the First Congress later described his "marvelous and exalted figure, kingly in bearing and nature. A royal scion of the House of David. Everyone sat breathless as in the presence of a miracle. It was the Messiah. The son of David. . . ." Once, when he had appeared in a street of the city of Vilno, throngs of Jewish people surrounded him, shouting: "*Yekhi hamelekh!*"—long live the king.

His audiences with foreign rulers bore little practical result, and his pleadings with Jewish millionaires were humiliating and pointless. But the enthusiasm he carried within himself was contagious and caused outbursts of ecstasy even in the minds of educated western Jews, however disciplined in restraining their emotions. Dr. Max Isidor Bodenheimer, later a founder of the Jewish National Fund, wrote under the impact of the teachings of Herzl:

> *The Zionist idea was the result of a sudden inspiration. It was like a light that suddenly broke forth within me. The remarkable character of this phenomenon shook my whole being. I felt like a slave for whom the road of liberty suddenly opened, like a prisoner who by a miracle finds a tool to break his chains. The state of mind into which this thought transported me can hardly be described. Whereas shortly before I had wrestled with the decision to abandon Judaism and seek refuge from Jew hatred where my origin was unknown, I was now filled with a holy zeal to serve the cause of my people. Perhaps it came from the fact that I suddenly recognized the futility of such assimilation for my people as a whole, perhaps also my feelings of honor resisted such a flight from the community onto which I was born. . . .*

Until the coming of Herzl, the longings for a revived nationhood had had the elements of a legend. But Herzl pronounced the significant phrase: "If you will it, it will not be legend." He succeeded in creating this will, which for centuries had lain dormant and now bore the abstract visions into the realm of reality. When he died, at the age of

The Central Zionist Archives, Jerusalem, Israel

Herzl's home in Hulda (taken in 1912)

forty-four, the Jewish world was no longer the same. Instead of a dream made up of mysticism, it now possessed an organized Jewish world movement equipped with parliamentary and executive organs. But, even at that stage, much of what he had accomplished still retained many of the elements of legend.

Chaim Weizmann, who later became the first President of the Israeli State, said, in Herzl's paradoxical style, "A Jew must believe in miracles if he is a realist."

The Central Zionist Archives, Jerusalem, Israel

Chaim Weizmann—six years old, 1880

Weizmann (seated, third from left) at the University of Geneva, Switzerland, 1903

The Central Zionist Archives, Jerusalem, Israel

Weizmann (middle row, third from left) with Zionist leaders in Kharkov, Russia, 1902

The Central Zionist Archives, Jerusalem, Israel

III

Pioneers from Eastern European Shtetls

But all these paradoxes and all these resolutions, the brilliance of diplomacy and the theatrical effects of the early Zionist congresses would have remained idle dreams in the pages of Herzl's utopia had it not been for the Jews of eastern Europe. It was they, the inhabitants of the Russian shtetl, who translated the oratory into practical deeds.

Confined in their gigantic ghetto called the Pale of Settlement, these Jews had lived for hundreds of years a traditional and rigidly orthodox life that had developed a peculiar concept of time. They lived in close attendance on the glories of the biblical past, waiting for divine deliverance in the future. Some Jewish historians, with an inclination to mysticism, saw the shtetls in terms of holiness: they were "sacred texts opened before the eyes of God." Others, with less metaphysical inclination, regarded them as places of captivity not unlike those of the captivity of ancient Egypt.

Until the nineteenth century, life in the shtetl was almost hermetically shut off from the rest of the Jewish world. Gradually, the good tidings of emancipation in the West began to penetrate the Pale. For the first time, some Jews began to think that perhaps here, too, even under the somber rule of the czars and the most reactionary of clergy, conditions might eventually change. And as in the West, they believed that the obstacle that stood in the way of such joyful fraternity with the Russian people lay not in the evil and superstition of the gentiles but in their own backwardness and stagnation. And they admonished themselves: "Shake off the dust, open wide thine eyes!"

They believed that as soon as a Jew shaved his beard, shed his Jewish garb, and gave up his hideous jargon forged from an already debased

German, the Russians would open their arms and clasp their Jewish neighbors to their hearts. Some of them went only halfway, proclaiming: "Be a Jew at home and a *mentch* [a human being] in the street." Others went after total assimilation, saying that the Jews had long since stopped being a people. "Nationhood ceased two thousand years ago; dead bones cannot be exhumed." Still others chose baptism, the "total identification."

Again, as in the West, the assimilationists and even those who chose baptism were bitterly disappointed, more bitterly than in the West. Their awakening came not just in the form of new anti-Semitic theories but in the much more tangible form of pogroms—organized by the police, carried out by the peasants, and condoned if not actually encouraged by the government.

During such a pogrom in the city of Odessa in 1881, Moses Leib Lilienblum, one of the leaders of Haskalah (Enlightenment), came out from the hiding place where he had escaped his would-be murderers with an undeceived mind: "It is not the different culture that is the cause of the tragedy, for aliens we are and aliens we shall remain." Another embittered Haskalah leader, Leon Pinsker, like Moses Hess in Germany, disagreed not only with the assimilationists, who saw the cause of all Jewish problems in their own backwardness, but with the socialists, who saw the remedy in a change of the social structure. "Anti-Semitism is a mental aberration which will not be eliminated with the help of rational remedies. The anomaly of Jewish existence can only be cured by getting to its roots. The mandate of the hour is not emancipation but self-emancipation in a land of our own." The pamphlet in which he formulated this idea was, indeed, called *Auto-Emancipation.*

Disappointment with the Enlightment and the shock of the pogroms led to the formation in Russia of groups of Jews who called themselves "Lovers of Zion" (*Ḥovevei Zion*) long before Herzl published his *Judenstaat.* The movement had a vaguely defined program: to promote emigration to Palestine with the aim of establishing agricultural settlements. In spite of the program, the movement still was not a party; it subsisted almost entirely on emotional drive. Nevertheless it was to write the first page in the history of the future Jewish state. It was from amid this movement that a group of students—thirteen boys and one girl—set out from the city of Kharkov and arrived in the ancient port of Jaffa, in Palestine, the first Zionist settlers in the Promised Land.

The Central Zionist Archives, Jerusalem, Israel

Leon Pinsker (1821–91), Zionist pioneer and author of pamphlet Auto-Emancipation

Statuts

pour

la Société

"בית יעקב לכו ונלכה"

"Viens maison Israel"

concernant l'organisation des Colonies en Syrie et Palestine, et soignante pour l'avenir de l'Emigration Israélite

§. 1.

But de la Société. Le but de la Société est de rétablir la situation politique-économique non moins spirituelle nationale du peuple Hébreu par colonisation en Syrie et Palestine.

§. 2.

Pour réaliser ce but, c'est que la Société tache à l'union de toutes les personnes qui rendent hommage à cette grande idée sans regard à leur état ou religion, et effectuera l'accomplissement d'un oeuvre basé sur la raisonabilité dans les pays ci-dessus mentionnés

§. 3.

C'est pour cela que la Société

The Central Zionist Archives, Jerusalem, Israel

The constitution of the Bilu, 1882

Conference of the Ḥovevei Zion leaders in Kattowitz, Poland, 1884. Standing, from left to right: Wollrauch *(London, England),* Pines *(Rosanna, Austria),* Deiches *(Kharkov, Russia),* Rabbi Friedmann *(Karlino, Poland),* Löbinger *(Kattowitz, Poland),* Luntz *(Riga, Latvia),* Dr. Rabbinowitz *(Paris, France),* Freuthal *(Kattowitz, Poland),* Davidsohn *(Warsaw, Poland),* Meyersohn *(Warsaw, Poland),* Dr. Pinsker *(Odessa, Russia),* Zederbaum *(St. Petersburg, Russia),* Rittenberg *(Warsaw, Poland),* Mirkin *(Poltava, the Ukraine),* Dr. Drübinowitz *(Rostov-na-Donu, Russia),* Rabbi Mohilewer *(Białystok, Poland),* Moses *(Kattowitz, Poland). Seated, from left to right:* Schalit *(Riga, Latvia),* Gordon *(Lyk, [country unknown]),* Jasinowsky *(Warsaw, Poland),* Friedenberg *(Białystok, Poland),* Friedländer *(Kattowitz, Poland),* Klewansky *(Kowno, Lithuania),* Dr. Chasanowitz *(Białystok, Poland),* Wissotsky *(Moscow, Russia),* Rabinowitz *(Warsaw, Poland).*

The Central Zionist Archives, Jerusalem, Israel

Some of the original Bilu members in Rishon le-Zion. From left to right: Eliyahu Sverdou, David Yudelevitz, Yehuda Zellechin, Moshe Meyerovitz, Shimshon Belkind, Pnina Belkind, Faynsberg (photo taken in 1922).

They were high school and university students from Kharkov, some of them not older than seventeen or eighteen. It would seem inappropriate to dub them with such a solemn name as "founding fathers," but this is what they were: thirteen founding fathers and one founding mother of a state that would come into being sixty-six years later.

The group to which they belonged was called Bilu, which constituted the initial letters of a passage in Isaish 2, verse 5: *Bet Yaakov lekhu ve-nelkha*—"House of Jacob, come, let us go." On their way to Palestine the group of young *biluim* stopped in Constantinople, where a manifesto was issued addressed to "our brothers and sisters in exile":

Nearly two thousand years have elapsed since, in an evil hour, after a heroic struggle, the glory of our Temple vanished in fire and our kings and leaders changed their crowns and diadems for the chains of exile. We lost our country where dwelt our beloved sires. Into exile we took with us, of all our glories, only a spark of the fire by which our Temple, the abode of the Great One, was engirdled, and this little spark kept us alive while the towers of our enemies crumbled into dust, and this spark leapt into celestial flame and shed lights on the heroes of our race and inspired them to endure the horrors of the dance of death and the tortures of auto-da-fe.

This spark is again kindling and will shine for us, a true pillar of fire going before us on the road to Zion, while behind us is a pillar of cloud, the pillar of oppression threatening to destroy us. Sleepest thou, oh, our nation? What has thou been doing until 1882? Sleeping and dreaming the false dreams of assimilation. Now, thank God, thou art awakened from thy slothful slumber.

The manifesto continues in this fancy language until the end, where it concludes with the brisk and categorical exhortation: "*We want a home in our country. It was given to us by the mercy of God and registered in the archives of history.*"

The first group of *biluim* was followed by others. This wave of emigration, known by the name of the First *Aliyah,* was followed by a second, this time made up not of starry-eyed intellectuals but of young radicals raised in the schools of Marx and Kropotkin. The pioneers of both *Aliyot,* however sustained by their zeal and idealism, were unprepared for the hardships and inexperienced in the conditions of work. The effects of the first two waves, which lasted from 1882 till the outbreak of the First World War, in 1914, were not very impressive: only twenty-one established settlements were scattered over Palestine, and the urge among the Jews in eastern Europe to follow in the footsteps of the first pioneers was minimal.

It seemed as though, the two first *Aliyot* having resulted in fewer than two dozen small, decentralized colonies, or *kvutzot,* this would have exhausted the enthusiasm of those who were willing to "get up and go" and that it would all remain an episode among similar utopian movements in the history of the Jews. But events in Europe created a new and more powerful "cause" for another wave of pioneers.

The Jewish Daily Forward, New York

Naphtali Herz Imber, Hebrew poet who wrote the "Hatikvah" ("The Hope"), the hymn of the Zionist movement. First published in 1886, the "Hatikvah" later became the national anthem of Israel.

The Central Zionist Archives, Jerusalem, Israel

First Zionist organization in Germany, 1895

The Central Zionist Archives, Jerusalem, Israel

Zionists, including Leo Motzkin, who, in 1899, helped found their first Berlin student society: Russia, 1895

The Central Zionist Archives, Jerusalem, Israel

Zionists: Bandar, Serbia, 1906

Actually, there were several reasons for this: One was the collapse of the czarist regime in Russia after the two successive revolutions that resulted in the disintegration of that "prison of nations." Another reason was the re-emergence of a sovereign Poland and Baltic states, which brought economic and political chaos. But the most stimulating and for the Jews euphoric reason was the news of the Balfour Declaration; of the official promise given by the government of Great Britain to establish a Jewish homeland.

Pioneers from Eastern European Shtetls

For the first time, the walls in many Jewish homes were adorned—besides the portraits of Moses, Rambam, Yehuda Halevi, and Theodor Herzl—with the portrait of a gentile, hitherto unknown and suddenly proclaimed one of the "Righteous among the Nations," Lord Balfour. Another new thing also made its appearance in Jewish homes and in many houses of prayer: blue metal boxes into which Jews would from now on drop coins for the Jewish National Fund with which to buy more land. In this way the Jews in the shtetl could participate personally in the redemption of the Land of Promise.

Zionists: Kamenetz-Polodst, Russia, 1901

The Central Zionist Archives, Jerusalem, Israel

The Central Zionist Archives, Jerusalem, Israel

Tzeire Zion ("Young Men of Zion"), a Zionist socialist youth movement that originated in Russia and Galicia in 1903 and, by 1911, existed all over Russia and eastern Europe. Here are Tzeire Zion in Łódź, Poland, 1910.

In shuls, when "called up to the Torah," they would make pledges of financial contribution to the same National Fund. Instead of wedding gifts, relatives and guests would offer sums of money to plant a tree in the Valley of Jezreel or in Galilee in the name of the married couple.

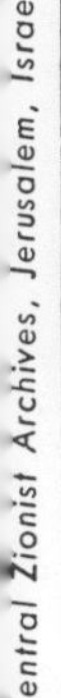
The Central Zionist Archives, Jerusalem, Israel

Zionists: Tehran, Iran, 1911

But the Zionist movement wasn't the only one growing up among the Jews in eastern Europe. The Zionists had to wage ideological war against other Jews, who were opposed to Zionism: against Jewish socialists, the Bundists, who believed that national distinction would lose importance with changes in the social system and that Zionism was diverting the hopes and energies of the people into other fields and thus delaying the final outcome; against the religious Jews who opposed their attempt to interfere with the will of God; against the assimilationists who insisted that Zionism aggravated the differences between Jews and their neighbors; and lastly, against a number of other Jewish leaders, who felt that any large-scale emigration would destroy the emancipatory progress that had been achieved and would produce a new mood of antagonism that would lead to new discriminatory measures.

But the Zionist movement kept growing.

The shtetl was caught between inner turbulence and the almost Messianic call from abroad. This time, many thousands were gripped by the urge to leave captivity and join those who were already in Palestine. But, this time, the experiences of the two first *Aliyot* had taught their lesson: be prepared. The new land was in need of idealism and readiness for self-sacrifice; but this wasn't enough: the land was also in need of experienced farmers who knew how to plow and plant; the wild stretches of land needed hands to cut roads; the country needed bricklayers, masons, locksmiths, and carpenters. Besides the spirit of idealism, the land was in need of muscle and experience.

Halutzim *on a farm on the outskirts of Warsaw*

The Jewish Daily Forward, New York

He-Halutz: Crimea, Russia, 1915

A new movement was organized: *He-Ḥalutz*—"The Vanguard." It was formed with just this aim: it was a group of training (*hakhsharah*) centers for future farmers and qualified laborers. The candidates were sent either to the private farms of Jewish landowners or to specially organized agricultural schools; also to co-operatives of various trades. The aim of the movement was formulated, in the spirit of the times, in flowery phrases: "to reach for the sky without leaving the ground of reality"; and still more picturesquely: "to harness the horse of Utopia onto the wagon of pragmatism."

Members of Ha-Shomer ha-Tzair ("The Young Guard"), a Zionist youth organization: Vienna, Austria, 1917

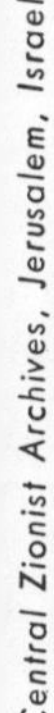

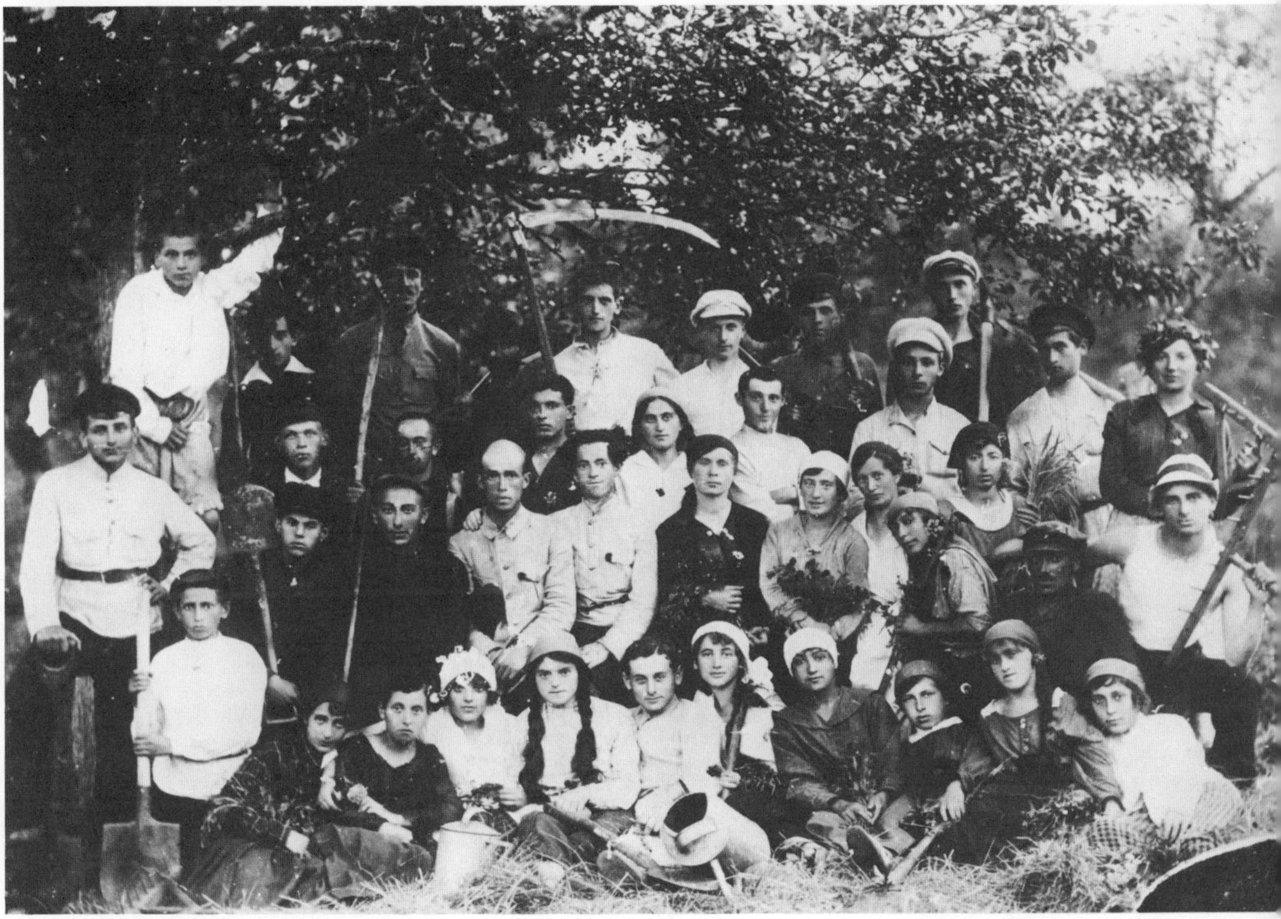

Hakhsharah: *Berdichev, Russia, 1919*

The Central Zionist Archives, Jerusalem, Israel

Leaving for Palestine: Warsaw, Poland, 1922

Herzliyyah, a Zionist group: Warsaw, Poland, 1922

Russian refugees in hakhsharah: *Lvov, Poland, 1922*

The Central Zionist Archives, Jerusalem, Israel

The Central Zionist Archives, Jerusalem, Israel

The training centers provided also intellectual instruction: the *ḥaverim* (members) of *He-Ḥalutz* received lessons in botany, geography, Palestinography, Jewish history, political science and, above all, knowledge of Hebrew, the language of the new land.

The departure of each group, after finishing the preparation period in the *hakhshara,* was an occasion for both drama and elation. In many cases the parents, even if themselves Zionist sympathizers, watched the departure of their children with apprehension. Where? Into a wilderness infested with disease and where superhuman strength would be needed. But, for the shtetl as a whole, the departure of a *ḥalutz* or a

Naḥum Sokolow presiding at the Zionist convention in Carlsbad: 1923

The Jewish Daily Forward, New York

The Central Zionist Archives, Jerusalem, Israel

Ha-Shomer ha-Tzair: Grodno, Poland, 1924. Poet Leyp Yafee is seated fourth from left.

group of *ḥalutzim* was the occasion of collective rejoicing. Everybody was caught up in a state of euphoria. The departing *haver* was farewelled with dancing and song. The departing *haverim* would carry, besides their meager luggage, gold-embroidered flags to be kept during the trip and, after arrival in Palestine, presented at a special ceremony to the *ḥaverim* already there.

But between the departure and the arrival lay a long road of unimaginable difficulties and tribulations.

The Central Zionist Archives, Jerusalem, Israel

Zionist Youth Conference: Pinsk, Poland, 1925

Ha-Shomer ha-Tzair: Slonim, Poland, 1924

Fishermen for Palestine: Poland, 1924

IV

The Journey and the Arrival

In 1903, Joseph Chamberlain, the British Colonial Secretary, offered El-Arish, a coastal town near the border of Sinai and Palestine, to Herzl for Jewish settlement. A commission of the Zionist Organization (shown

The Central Zionist Archives, Jerusalem, Israel

here) investigated the area, but the project never materialized, because of the refusal of Lord Cromer, viceroy of Egypt, to provide Nile water for irrigation.

Zionist tourists from Galicia posing in front of the pyramids en route to Palestine, 1909

The Central Zionist Archives, Jerusalem, Israel

In order to get to Palestine, one had to reach the port of Jaffa either by a ship that sailed from the Italian port of Trieste or by one that sailed from the Egyptian ports of Alexandria or Port Said. The problem was how to get there.

One way, if one started from Russia, was to board a boat in Odessa, sail to Constantinople, and then find another boat to Trieste. Before the Bolshevik revolution, this presented no insurmountable difficulty. And the Bolsheviks in the beginning of their regime shut their eyes to the existence of the Zionist movement and even to the existence of *hakhsharas*. Later, with the tightening of the regime, it became necessary to take the more dangerous way: crossing the Black Sea, illegally, in small boats.

Constantinople, Port Said, Alexandria, and Trieste could all be reached by land, although this was infinitely more complex and considerably more hazardous. The primary difficulty was "jumping" frontiers (crossing illegally); if you went one way, those of White Russia, the Ukraine, Poland, and Romania; if the other and longer way, those of Austria, Germany, and Italy, before reaching Trieste. This sounds very complicated, but words are weak to describe the reality of the ordeal.

Jumping a border required hiring a guide and bribing border guards. Very often the travelers were robbed by the guides, who into the bargain turned them over to the guards, and between them they took everything of value the victim possessed, which wouldn't amount to very much anyway.

Tired, destitute, and with no means, they would drag on with the journey; no wonder some fell sick and there were many deaths. In some towns they would be met by friendly Zionists, who would help; in other places camps were organized to provide the travelers with assistance.

The Jewish Daily Forward, New York

Olim *from the Caucasus, en route to Palestine,* 1921

The Jewish Daily Forward, New York

Whenever possible they took on odd jobs, any manual labor offered, just for a little food or a night's shelter.

The journey in such circumstances lasted many weeks, even months. One of the first of such groups to leave Poland, in October 1918, arrived at the port of Jaffa seven months later, in May 1919. They then traveled in the steerage of old, dilapidated, seldom seaworthy freighters, which often broke down or got stuck on sandbanks. The food, if there was any, was inedible; almost everybody suffered from seasickness. But even during those days and nights of misery, there were moments, like a lull in a nightmare, when the travelers would gather on deck and dance with joy and sing their hearts out. . . .

Olim *from Romania, en route to Palestine,* 1922

The Jewish Daily Forward, New York

But their tribulations weren't over when they arrived in Jaffa. The Balfour Declaration had been signed in 1917, but there was no organized, legal *aliyah* ("ascent"; i.e., to the Land of Promise) until 1920, and even then the British military authorities made all sort of difficulties even for those holding legal visas. Since getting such a visa required a very long wait and was largely a matter of luck, many of the young people were too impatient to bother with formalities. In many cases they were not allowed to land in Jaffa and had to go back to Port Said, Trieste, or Constantinople. In the winter of 1920 forty-five hundred such wanderers were stuck on all the roads of Europe, some in Egypt and even Syria (where they had gotten in on French visas), most of them camping in railway stations, in improvised hostels, some even in hospitals or prisons.

But in spite of all this, and in spite of the warnings from their own Zionist leaders, the *aliyah* didn't stop. In the year 1919, 1,806 entered

First pioneers to arrive in Palestine, August 1882. The boat that brought them over was named Thetis.

Archives and Museum of the Jewish Labour Movement, Tel Aviv, Israel

The Zionist Archives and Library, New York

Early Haifa

Palestine; in 1920, 8,223; in 1921, 8,294; in 1922, 8,685; in 1923, 8,175. Altogether, 35,183. As mere figures, this is not an imposing number, but, considering the background, it gains a different dimension. Of the over thirty-five thousand, 45 per cent were young Jews from Russia, 30 per cent from Poland, the rest from the Baltic states and Romania. All this demonstrates how marginal the role of Herzl and the other leaders from the West was compared to the impact of their practical followers from the East.

The boats that carried the early pioneers arrived at Jaffa, one of the oldest ports in Palestine and the world. The first sight of the Promised

Land did not resemble at all the romantic engravings in the Russian magazines. But they were too preoccupied with the enormity of their own vision to pay much attention to the squalor of the streets, the noise of the peddlers, the persistence of the beggars, or the suffocating smell of the bazaars.

On arrival in Jaffa many fell to the ground and kissed the dust. Others wept; still others broke into song, like Miriam after crossing the divided Red Sea. They were carried on the wings of their dreams, and Jaffa was only the gate to the real land, which lay beyond. The real land, too, was full of bizarre surprises.

Polish tourists in Palestine, 1923

The Central Zionist Archives, Jerusalem, Israel

V

Reclaiming the Land

Mikveh Israel, founded by Charles Netter on behalf of the Alliance Israélite Universelle, was the first modern Jewish agricultural undertaking in Palestine. This photo, taken in 1906, shows people harvesting in Mikveh Israel.

Archives and Museum of the Jewish Labour Movement, Tel Aviv, Israel

THE significance of the date August 11, 1882, the day of the arrival of the fourteen young *biluim*, makes it important to retrace their footsteps—the footsteps of the very first who set out from the Russian city of Kharkov to reclaim the "land registered in the archives of history." On their way to Palestine they were given, in Constantinople, the name of an already existing Jewish village that had been established four years earlier by the Alliance Israélite Universelle. The settlement had nothing to do with Zionist ideas. It had been an attempt of that French-Jewish philanthropical organization to rehabilitate a group of young religious Jews from Jerusalem who had decided to break away from a humiliating life depending on collected alms.

The fourteen *biluim*, carrying their meager bundles, walked the eight miles south of Jaffa to the village and told the manager of the agricultural nursery of Mikveh Israel (the Hope of Israel) that they wished to become peasants. The manager, Samuel Hirsch, in whose dictionary there was no such word as idealism, spoke to them with sarcasm and treated them with contempt. In order to drive out the "spirit of folly" from them, he gave them the hardest work and exacted it by brutal treatment.

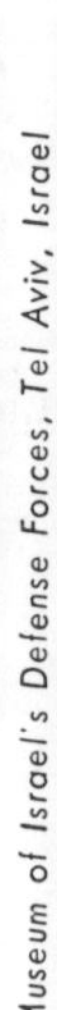
Museum of Israel's Defense Forces, Tel Aviv, Israel

A group of teachers and two guards in Arab attire: Mikveh Israel

Mikveh Israel, 1913

The *biluim* believed that after working an eight-hour day they would have time for intellectual pursuits. They soon learned the naïveté of this belief. Fortunately, most of them kept diaries, with the purpose of sharing their experiences with the "huge masses" who would follow their example. Here is a page of such a diary, written on August 21 by a Bilu member, Hessin:

> *We got up at five for the work, which would begin at six. We had no tea in the morning, fixed our beds, grabbed a loaf of bread, took our mattocks, filled our jugs with water, and strode for the fields with an overseer. There we took off our jackets, rolled up our sleeves and started digging. After a while my hands began to blister, the blisters burst, blood began to flow. The pain was so great that I was compelled to throw down the mattock; but I was immediately filled with anger at my own cowardice. Is that the way I want to prove that I am capable of physical work? Again I took up the mattock in spite of the piercing pain. I dug relentlessly for two more hours and threw myself down completely exhausted. The four hours seemed an eternity. At ten we took our belongings and went off to bathe.*
>
> *After we had bathed, the overseer brought us a basket of grapes. We ate and fell asleep. At 2:30, awakened, we were unable to work. All limbs weighed heavily, I felt depressed, but the living example of my companions lifted my spirit. They worked zealously and their spirit did not fail in the least.*

The overseers did everything to drive the spirit of folly from them, but the folly didn't depart and they persisted.

At that time, the Turkish Government had issued an order restricting immigration and forbidding the sale of land to Russian Jews. Then even more severe orders came from Jerusalem, that Russian Jews who sought shelter in Jaffa should be deported. The mood among the *biluim* became very gloomy. They had originally believed that their example would serve as a model for many other Bilu members who had stayed behind in Russia, that thousands of them would follow in the footsteps of the pioneers. A year after the first arrival, the number in-

The Zionist Archives and Library, New York

Biluim (*note the Arab kaffiyehs*) *eating dinner in the field*

creased slightly; they were still a pathetically small group: twenty-three young men and three girls, who occupied two small rooms in Jaffa. Only twelve of them worked in Mikveh Israel; the three young women kept house, some of the others carried on the correspondence, and a few simply pretended to be sick.

Their morale was at a low ebb and they began to think that all their sacrifices would end in complete failure. But just as everything seemed about to collapse, something quite unexpected happened. A group of Jerusalem Jews carried out a long-projected scheme and used some philanthropic funds to buy a piece of land southeast of Jaffa, where they founded a colony they called Rishon le-Zion—the First in Zion. The leader of the *biluim*, Samuel Belkind, pleaded with the leaders of the colony to allow a number of the *biluim* to transfer there from Mikveh Israel. The majority of the colonists were reluctant to

Harvesting grapes: Rishon le-Zion, 1910

The Central Zionist Archives, Jerusalem, Israel

The Central Zionist Archives, Jerusalem, Israel

Vineyard: Rishon le-Zion

admit these "dangerous Russian nihilists," but they finally submitted under pressure from Baron Edmond de Rothschild's agents. There the *biluim* had a close encounter not with the nature of man but with nature itself. What they got was dry, parched earth full of rocks; dunes, swamps, snakes, scorpions, bugs, and worst of all, malaria.

They came there with no working implements, no plows, not even seeds to sow. The most humiliating of all was that they had to live, until they gathered the first crop, on charity. The crop, because of the wretched earth and their lack of experience, was pathetically poor. But again they persisted.

The Central Zionist Archives, Jerusalem, Israel

Planting trees: Rishon le-Zion, 1890

The Central Zionist Archives, Jerusalem, Israel

Feeding chickens: Rishon le-Zion

Pruning vines: Rishon le-Zion, 1910

Delivering wine from Rishon le-Zion to Jaffa stores, 1911

Armed guards, responsible for defending Rishon le-Zion against marauders, 1910

The Central Zionist Archives, Jerusalem, Israel

The Central Zionist Archives, Jerusalem, Israel

Two years later, the leaders of the Russian Ḥovevei Zion movement held a conference in the city of Kattowitz and decided to settle the *biluim* in another newly established village in Palestine, in the South Judean plain: Gederah. On the second day of Ḥanukkah in the year 1844, eight young men went up to Gederah, seven *biluim** and one sympathizer. From then on, Gederah became a milestone in the history of Palestine, for it adumbrates the history of a great number of settlements to come.

* The names of the seven *biluim* were Solomon Zuckerman, Zeev Hurvitz, Jacob Mohilanski, and Jacob Liss, of Minsk; Jacob Solomon Chazanov, of Mohilev; Dov Leibovitz, of Ponevezh; Benjamin Fuchs, of Kherson. They were later joined by two more *biluim:* Elijahu Sverdlov and Menachem Mohilevski, of Poltava.

The Zionist Archives and Library, New York

These three girls, members of Bilu, helped found Gederah. From left to right: Sara Henkin, Leah Henkin, and Leah Hervit.

Museum of Israel's Defense Forces, Tel Aviv, Israel

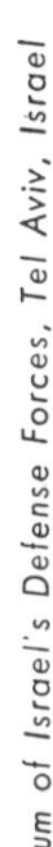

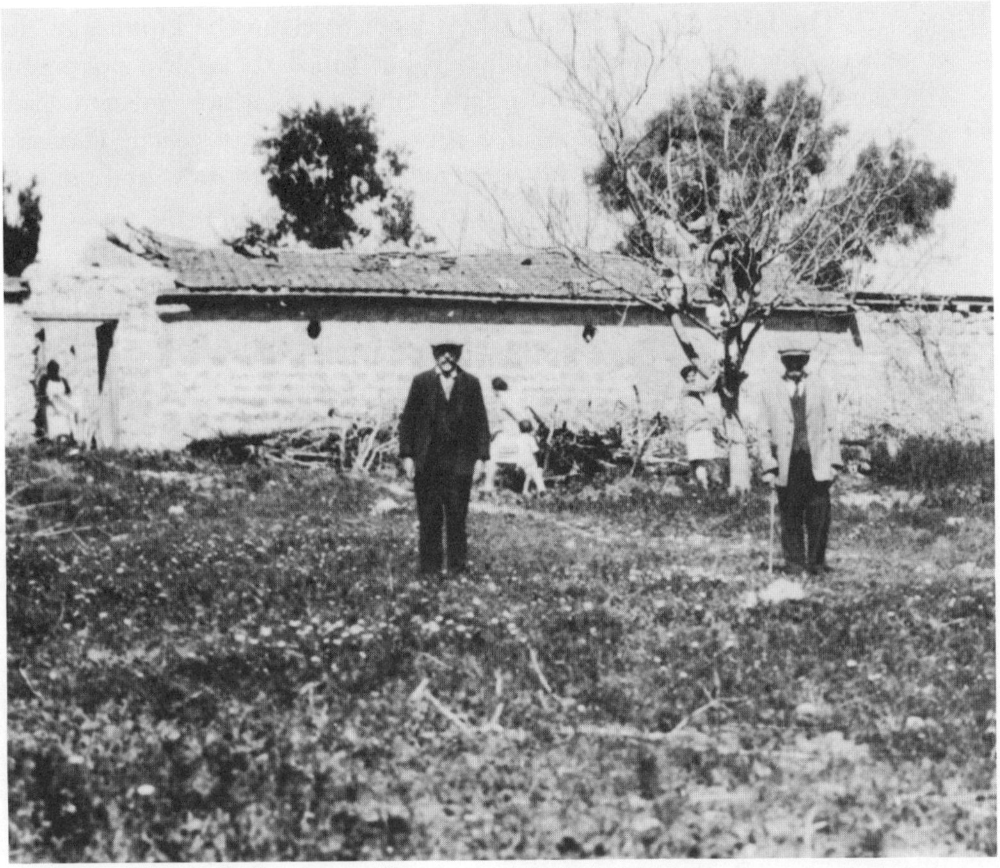

Gederah

To this new place they brought eight mattocks, one gun, one dog, one blanket, and a few sheafs of writing material. They built a small wooden shed five meters square, with three wooden benches along the walls, on which they slept. The middle of the floor was occupied by a wide table—at which to eat, read, and write, and at which in the evenings to express their overflowing joy in dancing. One of them, Yakov Shlomo Chazanov, later wrote in his diary: "Farmers! Be a free man among men, but a slave to the soil. Kneel and bow down to it every day. Nurse its furrows and then even stony clods will yield a blessing."

Coming Home to Zion

The first group of *biluim* who set out to claim the Promise of the Great One was followed by others. They called themselves not immigrants but *olim*, "those who ascend," pilgrims on a holy mission; each new wave of such *olim* was called *aliyah*, the act of ascension. The land to which they came was arid, neglected, covered with rocks and sand. It was a ravaged land, with the scars of a tragic history. In the eyes of the arrivals this was the fulfillment of the bleak predictions of the prophets! The punishment of God.

Petah Tikvah, the first moshavah, *in its early days*

The Central Zionist Archives, Jerusalem, Israel

Museum of Israel's Defense Forces, Tel Aviv, Israel

Harvest: Petaḥ Tikvah, 1900

The Central Zionist Archives, Jerusalem, Israel

Showers and tents for early settlers: Petaḥ Tikvah, 1910

In the new land, the newcomers met a strange phenomenon: The Arab villages were settled in the poor hillside country, while, to the incredulous surprise of the Jews, they found big empty stretches on the coastland and in the valleys, some with black soil even covered with greenery. Some of that land was eagerly bought, and at a low price, by organizations or philanthropists, but a year after the *olim* had built their settlements they found the reason for its emptiness: the soil they had bought was black because it was swampland, which meant the scourge of malaria. Some of the settlements, such as Petaḥ Tikvah, near the river Yarkon, and Rishon le-Zion, east of Jaffa, and Rosh Pinnah, near the valley of Ḥuleh, were built and then abandoned, and then rebuilt.

With the assistance of Baron Edmond de Rothschild, Petaḥ Tikvah eventually became a center of citriculture. Here are ḥalutzim, *in 1925, cutting trees.*

The Central Zionist Archives, Jerusalem, Israel

The Central Zionist Archives, Jerusalem, Israel

Rosh Pinnah, 1912

Private collection of Aaron Woulf, Haifa, Israel

One of the pioneers in Galilee, 1910

The Central Zionist Archives, Jerusalem, Israel

Back from threshing: Ḥaderah. Founded in 1891 by Bilu immigrants. The extensive swamps bordered by sand dunes were the source of malaria that caused the death of nearly half the settlers.

They clung to the swampland, even with its pestilence. Many died; the rest didn't give up. It was obvious that the swamps had to be drained, so they planted seedlings of eucalyptus trees, which help to dry soil by their enormous consumption of water; then they dug drainage ditches to draw the water into the sea.

VI

Three Aliyot

THE history, or rather prehistory, of the revived land is the history of five such waves of immigrants, of five *aliyot*. They started with the arrival in Jaffa of the young *biluim* in 1882. They and their immediate followers were mostly young Russian intellectuals, children of the Jewish middle class, who went to Palestine with the aim of establishing agricultural villages. Members of the First *Aliyah* (1882–1903) possessed tenacity and will power but lacked a definite program. Therefore, in the end, many of them became colonists rather than peasants, employers rather than the laborers. Their worst disappointment was not the toughness of the land and the harshness of the work; it was the apathy of the Jews in Russia, who didn't, as they had hoped, follow in great numbers.

The Second *Aliyah* (1904–14) brought a different type of *olim:* young revolutionaries who had participated in radical movements and were shocked when the Russian peasants, in whom they had invested so much sympathy and hope, joined in the pogroms, especially that of Kishinev in 1903. The new *olim* were disillusioned with the peasants but not with the socialist idea. They brought with them a new religion, that of work. They believed that physical work was fundamental to Jewish existence. Work was sacred, and the only thing that gave the Jews the right to the soil of Palestine was "the betrothal of toil."

Paving a road: Zikhron Yaakov

Plowing: Ben Shemen, 1910

Transporting wine barrels: Zikhron Yaakov, 1910

Museum of Israel's Defense Forces, Tel Aviv, Israel

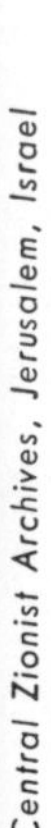

The Central Zionist Archives, Jerusalem, Israel

The Central Zionist Archives, Jerusalem, Israel

Deganyah A, first founded in 1908 near Umm-Juni by a workers' group from nearby Kinneret, was finally established on its present site in 1909. Jewish immigrants lived in Arab mud huts until 1911, when their number rose to fifteen and they built themselves personal housing.

Chicken farm in Deganyah, 1912

The *olim* of the Second *Aliyah* set for themselves two immediate goals: the establishment of self-supporting agricultural enterprises and the re-creation of themselves as laborers. In 1908 they organized a training center in western Galilee, Sejera, which was to prepare workers for other settlements. On December 9 of that same year, six young men and two women set out to build the first communal agricultural settlement, and called it Deganyah—cornflower.

The pioneers of the Second *Aliyah* proclaimed that the Jewish country should be built with Jewish hands. They were the importers of nationalism but at the same time of the idea of a socialist revolution. What they had failed to achieve in Russia, they hoped to accomplish in Palestine. There were no capitalists to fight, so the problem was not the redistribution of capital but, rather, the creation of an entirely new society.

Archives and Museum of the Labour Movement, Tel Aviv, Israel

The Central Zionist Archives, Jerusalem, Israel

Members of the Second Aliyah founded Kinneret, a training and experimental farm. Photograph taken in 1910.

Kinneret, 1911

The Central Zionist Archives, Jerusalem, Israel

Kephar Sava, 1909. The land was purchased in 1892. Baron Edmond de Rothschild tried unsuccessfully to cultivate the growth of medicinal herbs. While actual settlement began in 1903, it was not until the 1920s that the settlement began its rapid development.

The Central Zionist Archives, Jerusalem, Israel

Tents for new settlers: Kephar Sava, 1925

A family from Bulgaria in Har-Tuv, a colony in Bet Shemesh, 1911

Reḥovot, 1912

New settlers arrive in Lepuryah, 1912

The Zionist Archives and Library, New York

The Central Zionist Archives, Jerusalem, Israel

They also organized the group Ha-Shomer to defend the new villages, at first against lone marauders and then against organized Arab riots. Their ideals were inhumanly high, and many couldn't stand the strain. They broke under the self-imposed discipline, and a great number, almost 80 per cent, left. These either went home or emigrated to America. The Second *Aliyah* turned out to be a "survival of the fittest," not necessarily the fittest in muscle but in a power stronger than any physical strength, that of innocence. And those who survived became the core of the future state.

One of the first shomrim (*"guards"*) *in Galilee, 1905*

The Central Zionist Archives, Jerusalem, Israel

The Central Zionist Archives, Jerusalem, Israel

Shomer *in Reḥovot, 1910*

The Jewish Daily Forward, New York

Jewish cavalry acting as guards and rural police against attacks of Arab brigands in Palestine

Jewish shomrim *in Arab attire*

Baron Edmond de Rothschild with the oldest of the shomrim, *Abraham Shapiro, 1914*

The Third *Aliyah* (1919–24) began with the outbreak of the Russian Revolution and with the suffering of the aftermath of the war. This third wave was, again, different from the first two, which had consisted mostly of individuals, rather than of organized groups. Now they came in more imposing numbers and trained to face the peril and the disenchantment of the former two.

Founded in 1920 by pioneers from eastern Europe, Kiryat Anavim, built near Jerusalem, was the first Jewish agricultural settlement in the hills. These are the first tents and barracks.

The Central Zionist Archives, Jerusalem, Israel

The Central Zionist Archives, Jerusalem, Israel

Afula, 1920

The Central Zionist Archives, Jerusalem, Israel

Jewish pioneers on their way to a new settlement, 1922

The Central Zionist Archives, Jerusalem, Israel

Tent of a newly arrived family: Reḥovot

Building a new suburb of Jerusalem

The majority of the new wave of immigrants belonged to a political movement overwhelmingly influenced by Poale Zion ("Labor Zionism"), a movement that expressed a profound social concern and advocated the nationalization of land. A smaller group of the new immigrants belonged to Tzeire Zion—Youth of Zion. Some of them later joined the Poale Zion to form an enlarged *Aḥdut ha-Avodah*—Labor Unity. Still another movement that made its appearance at that time was a group that called itself *Ha-Shomer ha-Tzair*—The Young Guard—which had originated in Galicia in 1913 and been reorganized in Vienna in 1917. Their vision of a Jewish Home was deeply romantic and far more radical than that of the Poale Zion. In their zeal to reconstruct society they even preached the abolition of the family.

Other *ḥalutzim* came with a rebellious plan for group employment and formed upon arrival the labor battalion (*Gedud ha-Avodah*). Their aim was to socialize the *Yishuv;* they were prepared to work all over the land, in any region and under the most trying conditions. They didn't limit themselves to agriculture; their plan was to introduce Jewish workers into every sphere, such as road construction, house building, railway building and swamp drainage. Their further aim was to transform Palestine into a nationwide commune of Jewish workers. Everything they earned was to be turned over to a central body which would provide them with the barest means of sustenance. Their aspirations were too high, impossible to keep up, and the movement disintegrated. Some of them left the country, others began to settle in such communes as Ein Harod.

The Central Zionist Archives, Jerusalem, Israel

The Central Zionist Archives, Jerusalem, Israel

First family in Ein Harod. Shlomo Levi and his wife and child

Constructing barracks in Ein Harod, 1921

The Central Zionist Archives, Jerusalem, Israel

Naḥlat Yaakov, a Hassidic colony, built in the early twenties.

Women baking bread, 1920

Packing oranges in boxes, 1925

The Central Zionist Archives, Jerusalem, Israel

The Central Zionist Archives, Jerusalem, Israel

Cork factory in Tel Aviv, 1923

Pioneer lunch break, 1923

All the three *aliyot* were notable for the same pioneer spirit. The grimness of the land evoked in them only greater enthusiasm, challenged them to restore it to its ancient glory. No problems seemed insoluble, because the aim was not only reconquering the land but reconstructing oneself. To Ben-Gurion, as to many others who "ascended" to Palestine, it was an act of personal rebirth, and many counted the beginning of life from the day they set foot in this land.

The Central Zionist Archives, Jerusalem, Israel

This field, photographed in 1919, became Reḥov ben Yehuda, one of the busiest intersections in Jerusalem.

They came driven by a stubborn sincerity, by an almost superhuman sense of a self-imposed obligation. Of them the poet Ḥayyim Naḥman Bialik said that "the very dust will become alive under your bare and sacred feet." They were tough dreamers, because there is no greater force than lack of selfishness.

In the first letters they sent home, they enclosed blades of grass or petals of dried flowers. Few of those who received them knew their meaning: the grass and the flowers were born out of the entrails of a soil that had seemed to be dead. They were the symbols of a resurrection.

Other emigrants, too, have encountered a similarly hostile land and fearsome landscapes—in Arizona, Paraguay, Curaçao, and Rhodesia—but the pioneers in Palestine possessed a quality no others had: the conviction that they were revisiting an ancestral home. Everything was in a way familiar. It was from this much-heard-of port of Jaffa that the prophet Jonah had sailed on his ill-fated voyage. The mountains, rising ominous and destitute over the sea farther north, held the cave in which Elijah hid from the tyranny of Jezebel. Such places as Ashkelon, Gath, the mountains of Gilboa, were familiar to them from the Psalm in which David lamented the loss of his friend: "Tell it not in Gath, publish it not in the streets of Ashkelon. . . . How are the mighty fallen."

Jaffa road: Jerusalem, 1920

The Jewish Daily Forward, New York

Therefore, coming to Palestine was not another emigration, it was a homecoming. But the home to which they came was not quite as empty and deserted as many seem to have sincerely believed.

Ben-Gurion (1886–1973)

The Central Zionist Archives, Jerusalem, Israel

VII

Kibbutzim

DRESS ME, MOTHER

by Avraham Shlonsky

Dress me, mother dear, in a striped shirt of splendor
And at the break of dawn
Lead me to work.

My land is wrapped in light as in a prayer-shawl.
Houses stand forth like frontlets.
The roads we paved stretched out
Like phylacter-thongs.

A grateful city offers a prayer to its Creator,
And among those who created it
You can count your son Avraham,
Poet-saviour in Israel.

At dusk Father will return from his toil
And murmur a blissful prayer:
Avraham my dearest son,
All skin and bone and sinew,
Halleluiah!

Dress me, mother dear, in a striped shirt of splendor
And at the break of dawn
Lead me to work.

Translated by Abraham Birman

Avodah, the Hebrew word for work, has a double meaning: besides signifying work, it means to serve God. In the attitude of the early pioneers the dual connotations meshed: work became a cult and it was performed with religious zeal.

Those who arrived with the idea of becoming peasants did so because they regarded commerce and trade as aspects of an abnormal life, a deforming consequence of their long history of persecution. They came to Palestine to put an end to that; to reconstruct themselves into workers of the soil, an old romantic dream of the Jews, who had been deprived of the right to possess land. And also to show the world that the age-old accusation made by the anti-Semites, that Jews were inherently nothing but peddlers and moneylenders, tailors and watchmakers, was not true.

The young intellectuals, children of eastern European middle-class men or of small-workshop employees, had—to paraphrase the saying of Isaiah—beaten their books, notebooks, and pens into plowshares. As well as their will to make themselves over as farmers, they brought along rich utopian plans for creating an ideally just and unselfish society.

It soon turned out that building utopian villages was more than wishful thinking; it was also strict necessity. In that barren and swamp-ridden land, a high degree of co-operation gave the only hope of survival. The idea that lay behind the creation of the first communal villages was also dictated by economic needs, but their principal incitement was the Idea.

The Central Zionist Archives, Jerusalem, Israel

Building a new settlement

The Jewish Daily Forward, New York

Yeoman laborers in a kibbutz, 1923

Their first village, based on the principle of perfect equality and social justice, was built in 1909 on a piece of land, on the river Jordan, called Umm-Juni. A group of eight agricultural workers were given this lot by the Jewish National Fund, with the right to transform it into an agricultural settlement. The young men set out to do more than that. They decided to make this the first commune (Deganyah), under the principle of the abolishment of private property. Private trade would not be allowed; no money was to be used within the community; labor would not be hired; the whole group would assume responsibility for

Early settlers of Deganyah A, the mother of kibbutzim

The Central Zionist Archives, Jerusalem, Israel

The children of Deganyah

production and for all community services and individual needs. Marketing and purchasing would be done by the group as a whole, the profits to be plowed back into the future of the settlement. The highest authority was to be the General Meeting.

They also decided to limit the number of members to not over twenty, to preserve the character of an extended family. When later it happened that others wanted to join them, they organized a replica of the *kevutzah* (group) in the neighborhood and called it Deganyah B.

Deganyah was the first collective farm of its kind and for that reason was named the mother of *kibbutzim*. Others followed fast in its footsteps, sometimes expanding its size or changing some rules but always retaining its essential structure and character.

Life in the early *kevutzah* (*kibbutz* is an enlarged form of such a *kevutzah*) was austere and abstemious not only because of the poverty but because of the puritan demands voluntarily put upon themselves by the members. In the ascetic life they lived, even the smallest manifes-

Kibbutz Merḥavyah, 1910

The Central Zionist Archives, Jerusalem, Israel

The Central Zionist Archives, Jerusalem, Israel

Kibbutz Merḥavyah, 1910

tation of comfort was regarded with contempt. Golda Meir, the future Prime Minister of the Israeli State, who came at the time of the Third *Aliyah,* had great difficulty being accepted in such a *kibbutz,* for the requirements for new members were strict. She finally passed the tests and became a member of the *kibbutz* Merḥavyah, a *kibbutz* which, because of the malaria pestilence, had been built, abandoned, and rebuilt several times. Golda Meir writes in her autobiography that

> *. . . life was far from luxurious. To begin with there was little to eat, and what was available was dreadful. The staples of the diet were sour*

The Central Zionist Archives, Jerusalem, Israel

Kibbutz Merḥavyah, 1911

cereals, unrefined oil which we bought from the Arabs in goatskin bags making it as bitter as death, a few vegetables from the kibbutz's own precious vegetable patch, canned bully beef that came from British military supplies left over from the war and an incredible dish made up of herring preserved in tomato sauce. When my turn came to work in the kitchen, to everyone's astonishment I was delighted.

She explains that in those days *kibbutz* women hated kitchen duty, not because it was hard but because they felt it to be demeaning. Their struggle was not for equal "civic" rights, which they had in abundance, but for equal burdens. They wanted to do whatever their male comrades were doing: paving roads, hoeing fields, building houses, or standing guard—not to be treated as though they were different and automatically relegated to the kitchen. But she didn't feel that way about working in the kitchen.

> *I couldn't for the life of me understand what all the fuss was about and said so: "Why is it much better," I asked the girls who were moping or storming about kitchen duty, "to work in the barn and feed the cow, rather than in the kitchen and feed your comrades?"*

Golda relates how she began reorganizing the kitchen. After introducing, to the outrage of the others, some improvements in the quality of the food, she decided that

> *. . now something had to be done about the way we ate: our enamel tea mugs which looked so white and clean when they were brand new, became chipped and rusted after just a few weeks, and it depressed me even to look at them. So I went off and bought glasses for everybody. They were much prettier and much more pleasant to drink from. The herring also presented a problem. Not everybody had a knife, a fork* and *spoon; mostly each person had one utensil, either a knife, a fork or a spoon. The girls who worked in the kitchen used to wash the herring and cut it into little pieces, but they didn't peel off the skin and everyone had to peel his own.*

When she decided to peel the herring before they were brought to the dining room, there were complaints that she was introducing some of her "American ideas."

> *My most celebrated "bourgeois" contribution, however, about which settlers all over the* Emek *talked disparagingly for months; was the "tablecloth" (made from a sheet) that I spread on the table for Friday night suppers—with a centerpiece of wild flowers yet! The members of Merḥavyah sighed, grumbled, and warned me that I was giving the* kibbutz *a bad name.*

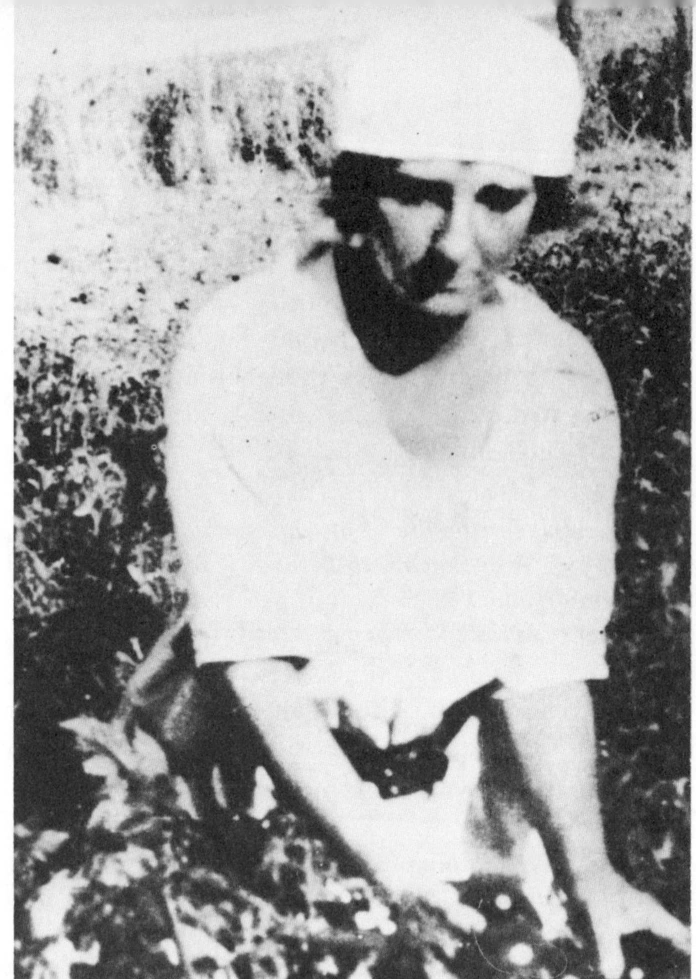

Archives and Museum of the Jewish Labour Movement, Tel Aviv, Israel

Golda Meir, member of Kibbutz Merḥavyah, 1921

Archives and Museum of the Jewish Labour Movement, Tel Aviv, Israel

But life in the communal villages created more serious problems than those. To begin with, the problem of families and children. It had been generally resolved that the family as a social unit should be liquidated, for it was nothing more than an "expression of erotic life." The idea that the two members of a *kibbutz*, a boy and a girl, should even think of forming a separate cell, preferring their own company to the greater family of the *kibbutz*, was considered unworthy of members of a collective.

Since the total abolition of the family proved to be unrealistic, one such member (let's retain his name: Shmuel Dayan, the father of the later, formidable, eye-patched Moshe Dayan), suggested that no *kibbutz*

Children's nursery: Kibbutz Ein Harod, 1921

The Central Zionist Archives, Jerusalem, Israel

Grandparents and grandchildren in a new settlement, 1921

The Jewish Daily Forward, New York

member should be allowed to marry during the first five years. But this, too, appeared too extreme even for Spartans. Young couples occasionally did form "petty-bourgeois cells," expressing, sinfully, their "erotic life"; and the consequent and unavoidable arrival of babies created a whole set of new and grave problems. The question was: to whom does such a child belong? Should the mother nurse it and bring it up as her own? In that case wouldn't such a child be private property, a thing which was against the very foundations of the *kibbutz?* Should a child be allowed to eat at its parents' table? Sleep in their room? Problems of that kind created ideological crises, but by degrees all demands that seemed to be too harsh for the nature of man were slightly modified and eased.

At that time, half the population brought by the three *aliyot* lived in such agricultural villages: *kvutzot* and *kibbutzim*. In the early twenties, another sort of co-operative was formed, a *moshav ovdim*, a collective farm that gave the members more personal rights to live in separate houses and possess private plots of land. But apart from these farms, which have molded the spirit of the young *Yishuv*, there was an equal number of others, workers of various professions and trades who were employed on building sites, public work, or in the developing towns. They, too, felt the same need of belonging to an organized group.

As early as 1897, members of various trades organized themselves into small local associations. In 1902 an event took place in Jerusalem that was the first manifestation of social struggle in the Promised Land: a strike of Jewish printers. By the year 1919, teachers, clerks, and railroad workers had organized themselves into associations that may have resembled unions. The need to create a central body was growing, which would co-ordinate the small associations already existing and include the many others still on their own.

In December 1920 a general conference was called in which eighty-seven delegates represented 4,433 voters. Because the delegates belonged to various political parties and represented diverse philosophies and views, debate was extremely heated and lasted several days. A resolution was finally adopted which became a milestone in the history of the country and, like the creation of the first *kibbutz*, was to mold the life of the new *Yishuv*.

The Jewish Daily Forward, New York

The Central Zionist Archives, Jerusalem, Israel

Kibbutz Ayelet ha-Shaḥar, in Galilee, founded in 1918 by members of Poale Zion

Beginning of Kibbutz Yagur, 1922

Tel Ḥai: 1920. The defense of this Jewish settlement in 1920 against Arab attacks became a symbol of survival and hope for Palestinian Jews.

The Central Zionist Archives, Jerusalem, Israel

The Central Zionist Archives, Jerusalem, Israel

Kibbutz Bet Alpha, 1920

The delegates voted to form a General Federation of Labor, called Histadrut, an organization that "unites all workers in the country who live from the fruits of their own labor without exploiting others." The purpose of the federation was to "arrange all the communal, economic, and cultural affairs of the working-class society" and "to create work and encourage immigration by building an independent labor economy."

And so the first three *aliyot* gave the *Yishuv* the first *kibbutz* and an organized working class, and also, in accordance with their program of building rural and urban co-operatives, created the first thoroughly Jewish city: Tel Aviv.

VIII
Tel Aviv

It all began in 1820, when a Turkish Jew from Constantinople, R. Yeshaya Adjiman, bought a house, in the Arab port of Jaffa, that came to be known to the Arabs as the Dar al-Yahud, the House of the Jew. In the following years, the house became a shelter for Jewish travelers and settlers, first for merchants and artisans, Sephardic Jews from North Africa, and later, in the second half of the century, for the first wave of Ashkenazi Jews, who called the port of Jaffa the Gate of Zion.

In 1884 the population of both communities, the Sephardic and Ashkenazi, reached five thousand. They were thronging in, under conditions of squalor and incessant noise; and into the midst of unpredictable neighbors who from time to time showed unmistakable signs of hostility. In order to avoid all this, the Jews withdrew to two quarters of their own, which they called *Neveh Zedek* and *Neveh Shalom*. The Second *Aliyah* swelled the Jewish community to seven thousand, and conditions became even less bearable. Then somebody had the idea of building a garden suburb outside the city, where one could relax in comfort after a day in the strenuous city. A committee was founded, *Agudat Boneh Battim*—Home Builders' Association, which deposited one hundred thousand francs with the Anglo-Palestine Bank in order to purchase, with additional aid from the Jewish National Fund, a stretch of land north of Jaffa that was really nothing more than a desert of sand dunes, and really nothing except a name: Karm-Jambal. There they proposed to build sixty houses for sixty families.

The Anglo-Palestinian Bank: Jaffa, 1907. This bank, established in 1903 by the Jewish Colonial Trust, became the central bank of Palestinian Jewry. David Wolffsohn, Zionist leader and founder of the Jewish Colonial Trust, is seated at center.

Founders of Tel Aviv gather, in 1909, to draw lots for land on the sand dunes outside Jaffa.

The founding day was set for April 11, 1909. On that day, immortalized by an extraordinary photograph that depicts a group of people gathered in the midst of nothing, one of them, so the traditional story goes, pointed to the ground and proclaimed that this was going to be the intersection of two streets, one named Herzl and the other Rothschild.

The announcement, according to another sanctified version, was made by Meir Dizengoff, the first mayor of a city that didn't yet exist, but whose own name would, some years later, be given to one of its main arteries. But, for the moment, the ceremony had all the appearance of a mysterious if not ludicrous ritual. Still more bizarre was the fact that the two nonexisting streets were to bear the names of two men who belonged to opposite camps.

The Central Zionist Archives, Jerusalem, Israel

Museum of the History of Tel Aviv-Yafo, Tel Aviv, Israel

Leveling ground for house building, 1909

Museum of the History of Tel Aviv-Yafo, Tel Aviv, Israel

This later became Dizengoff Street.

Theodor Herzl was the author of the utopian novel *Altneuland—The Renewed Old Land*, or "The New Land built on the ruins of the Old." He was a dreamer, but he knew that in order to fulfill his vision he must have a less utopian commodity: finance. On several occasions he tried his luck with the bankers of Europe: the Rothschilds. During one such meeting, Herzl, exasperated, said to one of the heads of the Rothschild family: "I have the brains and you have the money. Together we could fulfill the dream of a Jewish homeland." With talk of this kind his visits to the Rothschilds naturally ended in fiasco. The only one who did show an indirect interest in Palestine was Baron Edmond, called "the Dandy," who spent a lot of money to finance agricultural settlements. He did it, however, as an act of philanthropy and had nothing to do with that Zionist folly, which he vigorously opposed.

Later, long after death of Herzl and shortly before his own death, the baron said to Chaim Weizmann, the future first President of the future state, "Zionism would mean nothing without Rothschild, but so would Rothschild mean nothing without Zionism."

So the two, who had never been reconciled while alive, became close neighbors and met at an intersection in the heart of the first thoroughly Jewish city. But the association went even further. When it came to giving a name to this first Jewish city, Naḥum Sokolow, the Russian Zionist leader, thought of the name of Theodor Herzl's utopian novel and looked for a Hebrew translation of it. He found it in the writings of the prophet Ezekiel (15:3): Tel Aviv. Literally, Tel Aviv means the Mound of Spring, but a mound in archeology signifies a heap of ancient ruins. Tel Aviv therefore is the combination of the two words "ancient" and "spring," old and new; and so Herzl's utopian novel *Altneuland* became a reality.

Several days after the dedication ceremony in Tel Aviv, a gang of Jewish workers arrived with shovels and trowels, pitched their tents on the shore of the sea, and in the midst of blowing sand began to dig the ground of those first two streets. Sometime later, when the workers erected the walls of the first house, the future mayor, Dizengoff (to go back to legend) stood among them and pronounced what sounded to him a daring and fantastic prophecy: "Someday," he said, "this city will have twenty-five thousand inhabitants." It turned out to be the greatest understatement of his career.

The Central Zionist Archives, Jerusalem, Israel

Naḥum Sokolow

Within a year the sixty houses were completed; that same year, the foundations were laid for the first Hebrew *Gymnasium*, Herzliyyah. At the outbreak of war in 1914, Tel Aviv had 182 houses, surrounded, as was planned, with little gardens. During the war, the Turks, always hostile to the *Yishuv*, on March 28, 1917, ordered all the Jews of Tel Aviv (and Jaffa) to be expelled. Some of the evacuees were absorbed into Jewish settlements in the interior of the country, others got as far as Egypt and Damascus. In November of that same year, Field-Marshal Lord Allenby occupied Tel Aviv and the expelled Jews returned in triumph.

Museum of the History of Tel Aviv-Yafo, Tel Aviv, Israel

Laying the cornerstone for Gymnasium Herzliyyah, 1910

Museum of the History of Tel Aviv-Yafo, Tel Aviv, Israel

Opening ceremony of Gymnasium Herzliyyah, 1910

Museum of Israel's Defense Forces, Tel Aviv, Israel

Graduates of Herzliyyah in uniform of Turkish officers. In the center is Moshe Sharett (originally Shertok) (second row, seventh from left), future minister of Israel.

The founders of Tel Aviv on the veranda of Meir Dizengoff's house, 1913

Tel Aviv

At the time of the Third *Aliyah* thousands of new arrivals, having nowhere else to go, pitched their tents on the outskirts of the town, and gradually they became absorbed into the city. On May 11, 1921, Tel Aviv ceased to be a suburb of Jaffa and acquired the status of a municipality. From its very beginning Tel Aviv was unique among the cities of Palestine: it didn't have the holiness of Jerusalem, the exoticism of Tiberias, or the mysticism of Safed. Tel Aviv, which lies along the shore of the Mediterranean Sea and which from the beginning was settled by eastern European Jews, became, architecturally, a Mediterranean city inhabited by the restless spirit of eastern Europe.

Museum of the History of Tel Aviv-Yafo, Tel Aviv, Israel

Museum of the History of Tel Aviv-Yafo, Tel Aviv, Israel

This open field, where new immigrants pitched their tents, later became the busy intersection of Ben Yehuda and Allenby streets

The beginings of Sderot Rothschild, a village settlement, 1918

Sderot Rothschild, after it had been built up

Museum of the History of Tel Aviv-Yafo, Tel Aviv, Israel

Museum of the History of Tel Aviv-Yafo, Tel Aviv, Israel

The Central Zionist Archives, Jerusalem, Israel

The Central Zionist Archives, Jerusalem, Israel

Museum of the History of Tel Aviv-Yafo, Tel Aviv, Israel

A meeting place for writers on Tel Aviv's seashore, 1928

After World War I, Chaim Weizmann and chief rabbi return torahs to Tel Aviv, 1919

Leveling street in Tel Aviv, 1922

IX

Jews and Arabs in Palestine

JOSEPH EPSTEIN, one of the delegates to the Seventh Zionist Congress, a teacher and farmer of Palestine, took the floor and in the course of his speech used the expression "the hidden question." He referred to the question of the Arabs in Palestine. All the delegates appeared startled.

The year was 1905. Until then the problem of the Arab population in Palestine had been either ignored or minimized to the point of non-existence. In view of the fact that, from the very beginning, the thousands of young men and women who joined the early Zionist movement were great debaters, this sounds unbelievable. When one looks through the accumulated material of that most extraordinary period, one is amazed by the multitude of subjects that were raised by the early Zionists. Every aspect of the future state was discussed, argued, debated, analyzed in the most excruciating detail. What should the revived Jewish state be—secular or religious? Should it be organized on the principles of private property or of collective ownership? Should it be a land of agriculture or one of advanced industry?

But not once in those early days ot Zionism did anybody ask the very obvious question: "What about the Arabs?" How can the revival of the Jewish state be realized on a territory which, however sacred to Jewish hearts, had nevertheless been populated by the Arabs since the seventh century? Apparently, few of the young Zionists gave that fact much thought. The majority of them, as well as the rest of the world, regarded Palestine as a deserted and empty place. Theodor Herzl, who had visited it in 1898, wrote a detailed report without mentioning the Arabs at all. Four years later, he did mention their existence, but in his utopian novel *Altneuland*, which contains the most amazing and for that reason now one of the most quoted passages. When one of the characters in the novel, a Christian, asks the Arab chief, Rashid Bey, whether the Jewish settlers should not be considered intruders, the Arabian chief replies: "Christian! How strange is your talk. . . . Would you consider him a robber who takes nothing away from you but gives you something? The Jews have made us rich. Why should we be angry with them?"

The boy-scoutish reply of the Arab chief shows at least that Herzl was aware of the Arab presence. His closest political collaborator and one of the two principal speakers at the First Zionist Congress, in Basel, Max Nordau, is supposed to have said to Herzl, "But are there Arabs in Palestine? I didn't know!"

Whether this story is apocryphal or not, it demonstrates the ignorance that existed even among the top leaders. Is it possible that some of them consciously disregarded the Arab presence for political reasons? In view of all the facts that we have, this seems highly unlikely. The majority were, of course, aware of the Arabs' presence but seldom of an Arab problem. They considered it an issue to be resolved. The earlier-mentioned M. L. Lilienblum noted that there was indeed an Arab community in Palestine, but that it was small and backward; and once the Jews started settling in greater numbers, they would grow closer to each other and stop being strangers. The philosopher and essayist Aḥad Ha-Am went to Palestine in 1892 and discovered that the country wasn't empty; but he also noticed that the Arabs who inhabited the towns and villages were not at all concerned with Jewish plans and wishes. One of the few who spoke of the Arabs as a potential danger was the religious Zionists' leader, one of Herzl's forerunners, Rabbi Tzevi Hirsch Kalischer, from Posen, who wrote as early as 1862 not about the possibility of a rival Arab nationalism but about the peril of crime. "Would not the rapacious Arabs rob the Jewish peasants of their harvest?"

To some of the Zionists, the presence of the Arabs was, on the contrary, an aesthetic attraction. There was a trend among European poets and painters to idealize the romantic and colorful "sons of the desert." The poems of Byron and the writings of Victor Hugo had helped spread the mystique of the charms of the Orient among the Jews also. This reaching for romance added one more element to the general attraction of Zionism, an element of pride: after all, weren't the Arabs the Jews' first cousins? The descendants of a common ancestor, Abraham, who, by the way, was the first Jew.

Arabs in Beersheba

The Central Zionist Archives, Jerusalem, Israel

Rabbi Tsevi Hirsch Kalischer (1795–1874)

The Central Zionist Archives, Jerusalem, Israel

Aḥad Ha-Am (pen name of Asher Ginzberg), 1856–1927

The Central Zionist Archives, Jerusalem, Israel

Arab huts

When the early pioneers disembarked at the port of Jaffa, their first encounter with the cousins was somewhat of a letdown: The town was full of squalor; the inhabitants were noisy; the streets were filthy; still filthier were the bazaars, where the crowds of peddlers and beggars little resembled the romanticized portraits of Delacroix. Even in the villages, composed of mud-and-sandstone huts, the Arabs in their kaffiyehs and abayahs put one less in mind of the serenity of Bible days than of the misery and hopelessness of the eastern European ghettos from which the pioneers had just escaped.

The first contact on the personal level came in the form of an immediate conflict; the young Jews, totally unprepared to fulfill their idea of becoming "plowmen and planters," found that they would have to compete with Arab peasants who were experienced and could work

much better. The discovery was unpleasant, but one could learn to live with it. The Arabs were efficient and badly paid labor, and this gave some of the Jews, when the opportunity arose, a chance to exploit them, rather than to fear their rivalry.

Otherwise the relations between the Jews and the Arabs, considering their cultural and social differences, were not bad at the outset. The new arrivals lived with their Arab neighbors in the way neighbors live together all over the world: in an indifferent sort of peace and only a few fairly reasonable conflicts. Some of the early Jewish pioneers enjoyed imitating the Arab way of life by wearing their headdress and learning their ways of horseback riding and of handling a gun. Some introduced Arab colloquialisms into their language. There even existed instances of closer social contact: mutual visits to homes and invitations to special celebrations.

One of the early Hebrew writers, Mosheh Smilansky, was the first to write short stories about Arab peasants, presenting them in a most sympathetic and romantic light. If it happened that one Arab neighbor had sneaked into a Jewish colony and stolen an animal or a chicken, it was considered a natural thing to happen even among the most peaceful and friendliest of neighbors. There were also instances of passing animosities, but there was certainly no hatred of the kind the Jews had grown used to through the centuries they had lived among the gentiles.

But all this began to change. It slowly appeared that the Jewish *olim* were too much preoccupied with their own national revival to realize that a similar awakening was taking place among their biblical relatives. The first riots, which broke out in Galilee and in Jerusalem, and the bloody riots of the year 1921, came like thunder from a blue sky. Even then the seriousness of the problem was not fully grasped.

In their bewilderment, the Jews began looking in the wrong direction to explain the growing number of attacks in which men, women,

Arab members of labor movement in a May Day demonstration

Archives and Museum of the Jewish Labour Movement, Tel Aviv, Israel

Jews and Arabs in Petaḥ Tikvah, 1911

and children were slain and whole villages burned and plundered. The attacks reminded them of the pogroms in Russia and they considered them acts of anti-Semitism instigated by the Arab Christians, who like Christians all over the world had "sucked hatred toward Jews with the milk of their mothers."

Later the Jews blamed the mandatory authorities of Great Britain, who were shrewdly making promises to both sides. The British High Commissioner, Sir Henry MacMahon, gave promises of a national state to the Arabs, while Lord Balfour made similar promises to the Jews.

The Jewish Daily Forward, New York

The Jewish Daily Forward, New York

Arab guests at Tel Yosef, a communal settlement in the Valley of Jezreel founded in 1921 by immigrants from eastern Europe

Street scene between Jews and Arabs in Tel Aviv

Putting the blame on others helped them little to face the rising tide of growing Arab nationalism. The Jewish pioneers who came equipped with zeal and devotion, but also with complete innocence, were profoundly confused. This no longer was a "hidden question"; it came out into the open and began to figure increasingly on the agendas of Zionist meetings and congresses, slowly coming to occupy the very top. With the unveiling of the "hidden question," the problem no longer was who was to blame but what was to be done?

All the theories of the past proved irrelevant and ineffective. Herzl himself, in the rare moments when he did talk about it, was convinced that the Arabs would be glad to trade nationalism for an improved standard of living. Another solution was seen in the hope that economic collaboration would act as a stimulant to political reconciliation. The Russian Zionist leader Naḥum Sokolow believed that the rapprochement with the Arabs would be achieved in the area of culture. He advised the Jews to draw nearer to the Arabs in order to build together a great Palestinian civilization.

At the time of the earlier settlements, Arthur Ruppin, a German Zionist leader who represented the Zionist movement in the Palestine office in Jaffa, suggested a most ingenious solution: a territorial transfer. The Arab peasants, who were dispossessed after the Jews had bought the land from their absent effendis, could be transferred to territories in northern Syria acquired by Jewish funds. Another Zionist leader, Leo Motzkin, extended the transfer plan, suggesting the resettlement of the Arabs in more places outside Palestine.

There were others, like the Marxist Zionists, who didn't bother with the nationalism of either the Jews or the Arabs. Since the ultimate aim was the establishment of a proletarian supranational society, the matter of nationalism was only a passing phenomenon and therefore irrelevant. Other Marxists, with a flair for scholastic "pilpul," argued, again drawing from the teachings of their master, that since the Arabs were devoid of economic or cultural characteristics, it therefore followed that even if they insisted, they could not be considered a nation.

To complicate matters further, there were a number of Arab notables who, for a variety of reasons, came out in defense of Zionism. Some of them went as far as to quote the Koran in order to prove that the Jews indeed had a right to return, and they proclaimed that "as brothers we shall live together." Chaim Weizmann, the future first Pres-

The Central Zionist Archives, Jerusalem, Israel

Chaim Weizmann and Prince Feisal, 1918

ident of the Jewish state, concluded a treaty with Prince Feisal of Arabia (later, king of Iraq) in which Feisal declared that, "mindful of racial kinship," Palestine should be opened to Jewish immigration, while two states, Arab and Jewish, should be created simultaneously.

All these solutions, flowing from naïveté, wishful thinking, or a blind national egocentricity, didn't help to diminish the militancy of the Arabs and the growing confusion of the Jews. Zionist leaders began using a more sober vocabulary. In 1917, Harry Sacher, a close collaborator of Weizmann, said that "even if all our political scheming will work out well, Arabs will remain a tremendous problem." Four years later, for the first time there emerged the ultimate, frightful foreboding. One of the delegates to the Twelfth Zionist Congress spoke openly about the "threat of an all-out war."

The Third *Aliyah*, with which ends the story of this book, left Palestine with eighty-five thousand Jewish settlers. At this point the struggle with nature began to shift to a secondary stage, to a struggle with the nature of man. There are many who have asked the question: What would have happened if the fathers of Zionism had possessed more foresight and the pioneers less unawareness? Would they still have set out on this daring venture? But such a question is no longer relevant.

Jewish and Arab members of Workers Club: Haifa, 1924

Arab shomer *in his traditional attire*

By the end of the Third *Aliyah,* a new troupe was waiting in the wings, Polish Jews who had been ruined by economic calamities deliberately produced by an anti-Semitic government. And a step behind this Fourth, a Fifth *Aliyah* was getting ready to come, the most tragic of them all: the lonely survivors of a whole people who had been destroyed by fellow humans.

X

Renewing the Holy Language in the Holy Land

A Bokharan Jewish woman in the Bokharan Quarter of Jerusalem

The Jewish Daily Forward, New York

WHEN the first groups of the *biluim* were on their way from Constantinople to Jaffa, the cultural picture of Jewish Palestine was one of utter confusion. It was, to draw a parallel from biblical stories, a Tower of Babel, where the Jewish inhabitants spoke, if not seventy languages, at least a dozen. The majority of the twenty to twenty-five thousand Jews of the Old *Yishuv* (old settlement—to distinguish them from the new) lived within the walls of the Old Jerusalem; others were scattered over such holy cities as Safed, Tiberias, and Hebron; still others in the more predominantly Arab cities of Haifa and Jaffa.

The settlers consisted for the most part of Ashkenazim (Jews who had come from eastern Europe) and of Sephardim (Spanish and Portuguese Jews, who after their exile from Spain in 1492 settled in north African countries and in the Balkans, Turkey, and many parts of the Ottoman Empire).

The Ashkenazi Jews kept coming throughout the fifteenth, sixteenth, and seventeenth centuries, most of them individually, with the purpose of praying, fasting, and then waiting for the day of death. The first-organized and largest group of Ashkenazi Jews were disciples of the founder of the Ḥasidic movement, the Baal Shem Tov, who had himself wished to come to the Holy Land but was unable to do so. His disciples came, then, in the eighteenth century, to fulfill his dream. Another group, of a different nature, were the disciples of the Vilna Gaon, an opponent of the *Ḥasidim*. His followers, called the *Perushim*, settled in Jerusalem in 1808, forming another community.

The Jewish Daily Forward, New York

Sephardic Jews at the Wailing Wall, in Jerusalem

Persian Jews in Jerusalem

The Central Zionist Archives, Jerusalem, Israel

A shopkeeper in the most religious quarter of Jerusalem, Me'a She'arim ("One hundred gates")

Elderly Jews in the ancient town of Safed

The Jewish Daily Forward, New York

The Jewish Daily Forward, New York

Street beggars in Jerusalem

Most of the Ashkenazi Jews lived in terrible poverty, depending on charity from abroad. They were aliens, not recognized by the Turkish authorities. They spoke Yiddish among themselves, and even on the soil of the Holy Land they lived like the poorest of the poor in the ghettos of eastern Europe.

The Sephardim were equally pious but socially more advanced. Some of them were artisans and small merchants and had the status of Turkish citizens. They brought along a language called *Ladino*, a medieval Spanish heavily intermixed with Hebrew and written with Hebrew characters. They also spoke Arabic and some even Turkish, and of course Hebrew, which they pronounced differently from the Ashkenazim.

A Sephardic Jew at the spinning wheel

The Jewish Daily Forward, New York

There was also in Jerusalem at that time a community of several hundred Jews who had come from Yemen. These had begun arriving in the fifteenth century, some of them yearning to live in the legendary land of the Bible, but also if not mainly to escape the inhuman conditions in which they were forced to live in their own country, trampled underfoot by their Muslim neighbors and subjected to constant humili-

The Jewish Daily Forward, New York

Yeminite boy

The Central Zionist Archives, Jerusalem, Israel

Yemenite rabbis

ations and threats. After the Turkish conquest of Yemen, which the Turks were to rule off and on for four hundred years, communication between Palestine and Yemen ceased, and in the years 1882–84, at the exact same time when the small groups of Jewish students from the Russian cities of Kharkov and Odessa "got up to go," Yemenite Jews, too, began to arrive—from the opposite direction and under even more disastrous conditions.

The Jewish Daily Forward, New York

Yemenite Jews

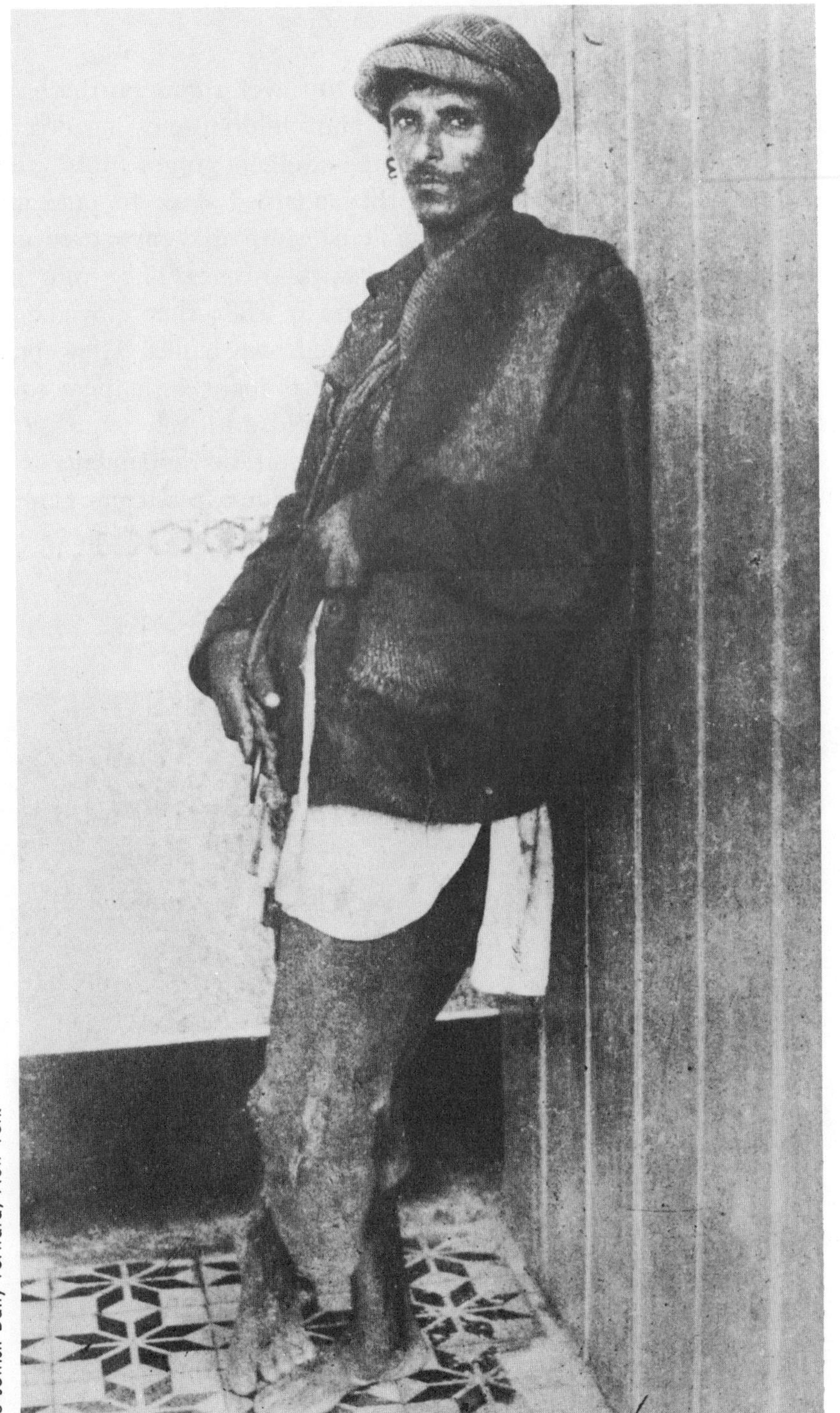

The Jewish Daily Forward, New York

It took them long weeks and months to travel, riding on the backs of camels and donkeys with their wives and children, crossing deserts, climbing mountains, and fording water-swollen gorges until they reached the port of Hodeida, where they boarded ships to Jaffa and from there proceeded on foot to Jerusalem. Most of them settled outside the old walls and lived in the biblical way—in caves. They were supported by various charity organizations, and in 1885 they moved to a Jerusalem suburb, into houses built with their own hands. They spoke Arabic with a sprinkling of Hebrew and had brought with them some professional skills, mostly those of tinsmith, goldsmith, silversmith, saddler, and cobbler. When the first Jewish agricultural settlements were started, many of them went there to work as builders, plasterers, carpenters, or welders in Reḥovot, Rishon le-Zion, and Petaḥ Tikvah.

Olim *from Iraq*

The Central Zionist Archives, Jerusalem, Israel

Apart from these distinct Jewish groups, the Old *Yishuv* contained others, who came from as far away as Afghanistan, Bokhara, and the Caucasus, as well as from Tunisia, Ethiopia, Iraq, Libya, and Egypt. An even more exotic group was a community of Shomronim (Samaritans), who claimed to be the descendants of the Jews of the ancient capital of the kingdom of Israel, Shomron (Hellenized as Samaria), who had once quarreled with the others, from the kingdom of Judah, about the selection of Mount Moriah as a site for the Temple instead of their sacred mountain of Gerizim.

Jews from India

The Central Zionist Archives, Jerusalem, Israel

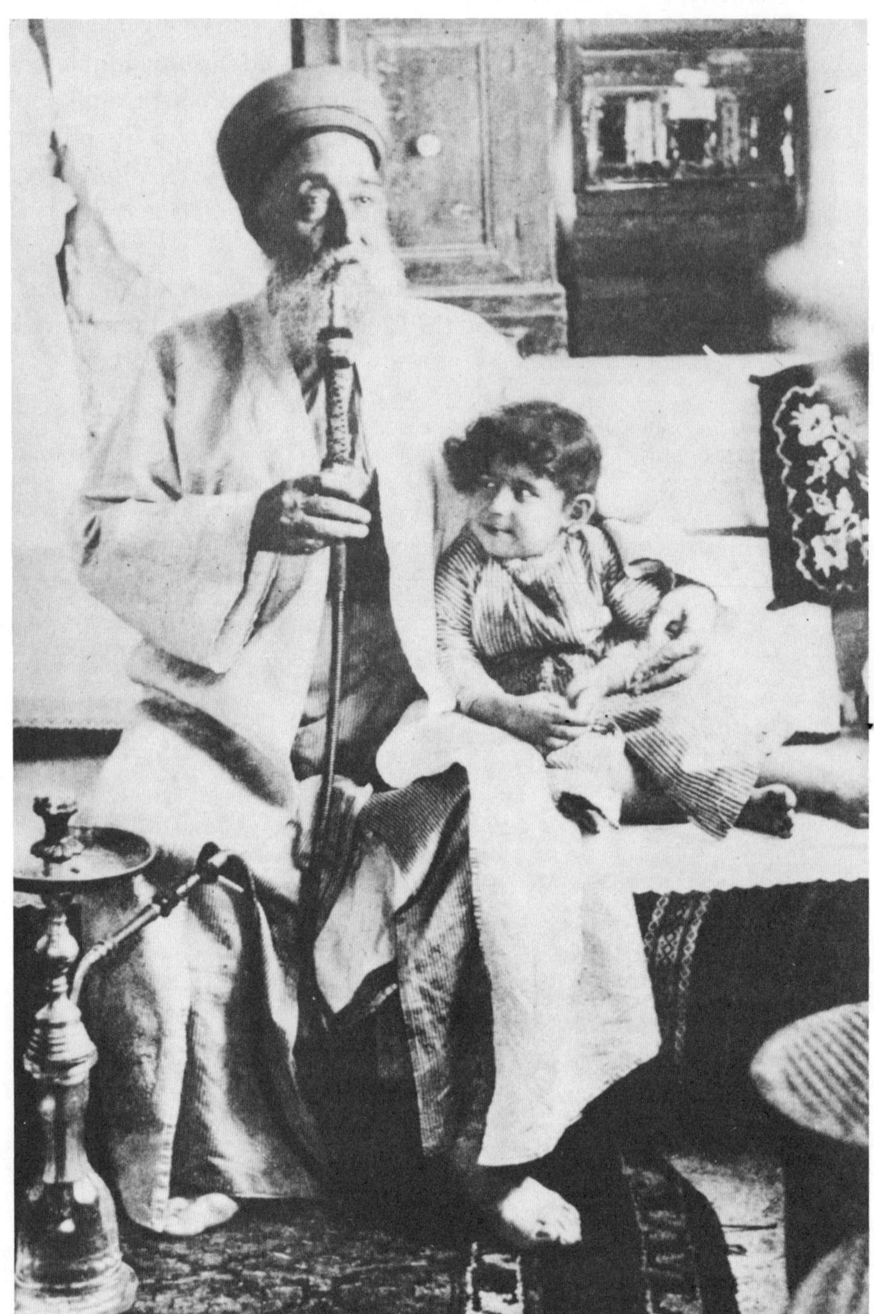

The Jewish Daily Forward, New York

The high priest of the Samaritans

In short, when the first pioneers stepped onto the shores of their Promised Land and took their first look at the variety of Jews already there, they saw the fulfillment of the divine promise of the ingathering of the Jews.

The differences in culture and background were reflected in the kinds of education that each of these groups had given their children. The Ashkenazim, pious and rigidly orthodox, had simply continued the kind of religious instruction they had brought from the shtetl. The younger children were sent to the primary school, the *ḥeder*, the older to Talmud Torahs and *yeshivot*. All the subjects taught were religious; the textbooks were the Bible and the Talmud. These were read in the original Hebrew and Aramaic and translated into Yiddish.

The Sephardic community also had schools of religious instruction (the *kutub*), where the Bible and Talmud, read with a different Hebrew pronunciation, were translated into Ladino and Arabic. All these religious schools were for boys only; girls were excluded.

But, at the same time, a network of other schools, of a more secular nature, were scattered over the land. They were established and supervised by Jewish philanthropical organizations abroad. At that time a great part of the area that is now called the Middle East was part of the Ottoman Empire, and various European countries carried on a struggle for cultural supremacy there. The most active were the Germans and the French, and at first these endeavors were undertaken by individuals, rather than groups.

The Jewish Daily Forward, New York

Yeshivah boys of Jerusalem

In 1856 a school existed in Jerusalem that had been established by an Austrian Jew named Simon von Lämel and where the subjects, both religious and secular, were taught in German. Then, in 1864, a member of the French branch of the Rothschild family in France, Evelina de Rothschild, opened a school that aroused violent opposition, for its teaching was secular, taught in French and, worst of all, for girls. The school was eventually taken over by an Anglo-Jewish association and the language of instruction changed from French to English.

Very soon, these individual endeavors were taken over by strong and well-organized groups, the French Alliance Israélite Universelle and the German Hilfsverein der Deutschen Juden.

The Alliance had been founded in 1860 by a group of French Jewish businessmen and intellectuals with headquarters in Paris. Their aim was to promote vocational training among backward Jewish communities; one of the results of their work was the agricultural school in Palestine, Mikveh Israel, in 1870, the first workplace for the 13 *biluim* from Kharkov. Along with their philanthropical work among the poor, the Alliance also established schools, in Jerusalem, Tiberias, Safed, and Haifa, that used French as a medium of instruction.

A school for girls: Jaffa, 1870

Teachers Seminary, founded by the "Ezra" organization: Jerusalem, 1904

At the same time, another philanthropic organization was founded by German Jews, which bore the simple name Hilfsverein (Ezra in Hebrew) and began to work at the beginning of the century with a similar purpose of giving assistance to the poor and German culture to anybody who desired it. They managed to open more schools than the Alliance, and in 1931 were operating twenty-seven such schools, from kindergartens to a teacher-training college, where German was the chief language but where Hebrew was also taught, at least in some of them, by competent teachers.

Renewing the Holy Language in the Holy Land

With the arrival of the first Jewish pioneers, the number of languages spoken and taught among the Jews in Palestine—two different Hebrews, Yiddish, Arabic, Ladino, German, English, and French—increased. The new arrivals added White Russian, Russian, Ukrainian, Polish, Lithuanian, and Romanian. But these early pioneers, who came determined to revive the land, also brought along an equally strong determination to revive the ancient language, which had been exiled along with its people and, like its people, was in need of redemption.

Kindergarten: Jerusalem, 1907

The Central Zionist Archives, Jerusalem, Israel

Such an impossible task would require inspired and persistent individuals with superhuman perseverance and total devotion, and such a man was found in Eliezer Perlemann, a Lithuanian Jew, born in 1858, who had changed his name to Eliezer Ben-Yehudah. He went to Palestine in 1881 (a year before the prologue of the First *Aliyah*) with one purpose: to fight for the transformation of Hebrew into a living and spoken language.

His methods were as forcible as his aims. On the boat between Marseilles and Jaffa, he announced to his wife that from now on their conversations would be conducted solely in Hebrew. It cut down considerably on their communication but increased their fluency in the language. They settled in Jerusalem, and when his wife, the following year, gave birth to a boy, he decided that the son would be exposed to no other language than Hebrew. Nobody who spoke another language was admitted to the boy's presence. This caused some difficulties in bringing him up, but he became the first Palestine-born, Hebrew-speaking child.

The most important and historic decision of Ben Eliezer, however, was not the choice of Hebrew over other tongues but between the Hebrews spoken by the Ashkenazim and by the Sephardim. The difference lies in the pronunciation. The Ashkenazi Hebrew is soft, flexible, and mellow; the accent of the words falls on the second-last syllable, as in the Slavic languages. Sephardic Hebrew is almost monosyllabic: abrupt, energetic, and virile. Ben-Yehudah, who had more sympathy in general with the Sephardic way of life, chose the latter, believing that the Ashkenazic pronunciation should be discarded along with other aspects of the Diaspora.

In 1897 he and a few others created a secret society, Tehiyyat Israel (Revival of Israel), whose members solemnly swore that from then on they would speak only Hebrew to each other, "even in such delicate situations as the open market." The very idea of starting a secret group of this kind, in a country where the language was not forbidden, where nobody had to go underground to speak it, and where there was no danger of violence when it was used in the marketplace, demonstrates the character, the style, and the spirit of the Father of Modern Hebrew.

Despite failing health, he took upon himself the formidable task of creating—all by himself—a dictionary of Hebrew and of inventing the words that the biblical and talmudic vocabularies didn't possess. He

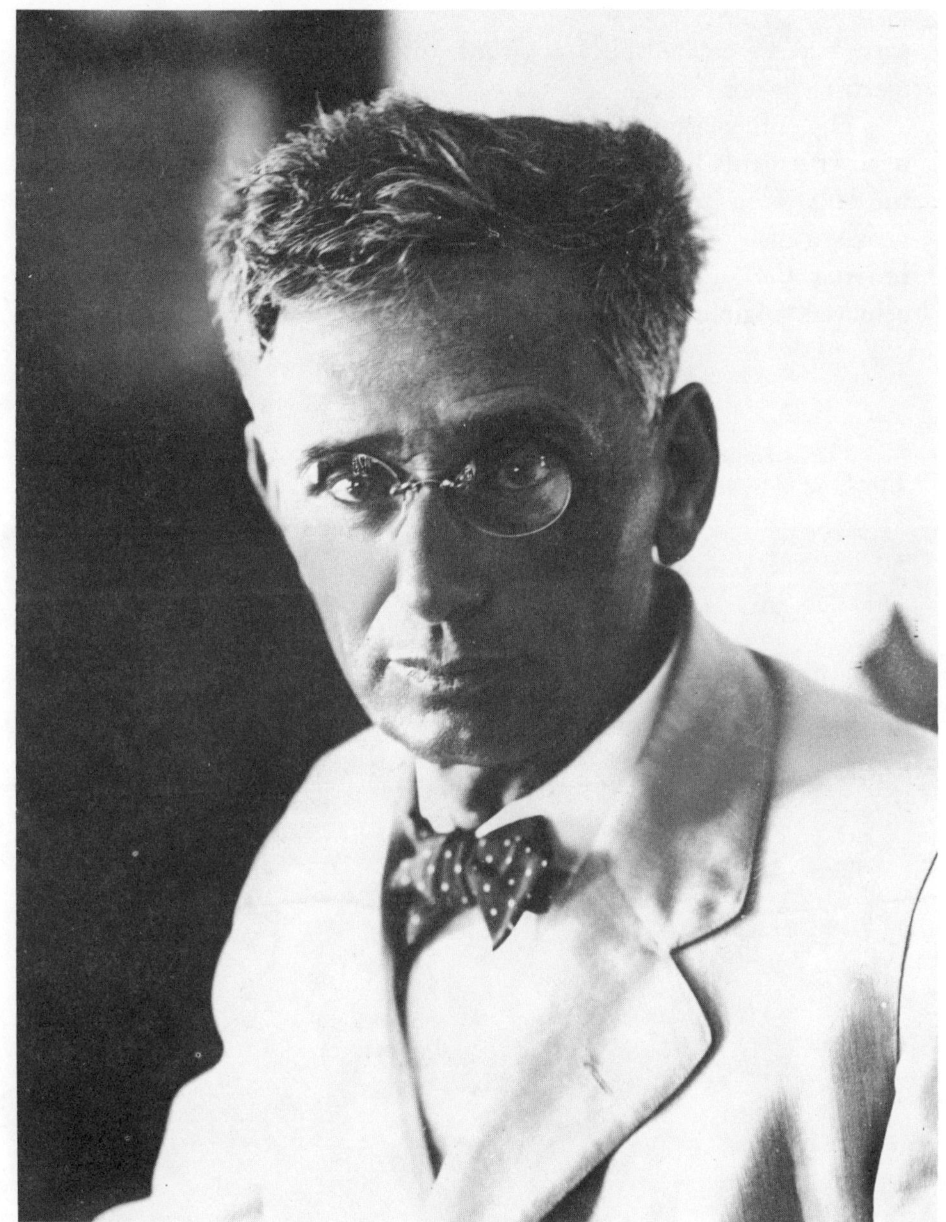

Eliezer Ben-Yehudah (originally Eliezer Perlemann), 1858–1922

even had to create the very word "dictionary," *milon,* from *milah,* meaning "word."

His enthusiasm, stamina, and persistence were contagious. All the new settlements became laboratories, where the pioneers were willing at the end of an arduous workday to speak the imperfectly known language to each other. The whole *Yishuv* was caught up in this dream of reviving the old language. Soon the perseverance of the first few achieved tangible results.

Teaching Hebrew to adults, 1910

The Central Zionist Archives, Jerusalem, Israel

The Jewish Daily Forward, New York

A Hebrew school in the Valley of Jezreel

By 1888 the school in Rishon le-Zion taught all its subjects in Hebrew. By 1892 similar primary Hebrew schools had sprung up in all parts of the country. By 1903 a conference of Hebrew teachers in Zikhron Yaakov laid the foundations of a teachers' association to help draw up syllabuses and publish textbooks and educational material for teachers.

The most arduous task was to change the biblical language (the whole Bible has no more than 7,704 words) into a fluent, colloquial language that included all scientific and technological terms. A special conference was called in 1904, which formed the Vaad ha-Lashon ha-Ivrit (Hebrew Language Council), both to revive the old words and to create new.

The Jewish Daily Forward, New York

Yemenite teacher in Rishon le-Zion, 1923

In 1906, the first Hebrew secondary school, the Gymnasium Herzliyyah, was founded in Haifa (later, in 1909, transferred to Tel Aviv). A similar school was established in Jaffa. In 1897 the First Zionist Congress, in Basel, had heard mention of a remote, romantic possibility: the establishment of a Hebrew university in Jerusalem. The Fifth Congress, in 1901, passed a resolution, submitted by Chaim Weizmann, "advocating to examine the possibility of establishing a Hebrew College for Higher Studies." In 1914, an area of land on Mount Scopus, in Jerusalem, was purchased by the Lovers of Zion, in Odessa. In July 1918, the foundation stone was laid by Chaim Weizmann. The official opening took place seven years later, the ceremony being performed by Lord Balfour himself.

The Central Zionist Archives, Jerusalem, Israel

David Wolffson, seated third row, sixth from right, visits Gymnasium Herzliyyah: Tel Aviv, 1917

As it turned out, however, the first Hebrew institution for higher learning was not to be the University, in Jerusalem, but the Technion, a technological school in Haifa. The origin of this school is connected with a most bizarre mass demonstration and a rebellion that is perhaps unique in the history of educational institutions. The idea for such a school came from the German-speaking Hilfsverein. The money was provided mostly by two Jewish philanthropists: Kalonymos Wissotzky, from Moscow (who gave one hundred thousand rubles), and the American Jacob Schiff, who gave an equal amount but in American dollars. The rest was raised from Jewish contributions all over the world.

The Technion (Israel Institute of Technology), in Haifa, 1913

The Hilfsverein proceeded to construct the building on the slopes of Mount Carmel, in Haifa. As they had a majority on the board of directors, the members of the Hilfsverein assumed that the language of instruction would be German. How could one teach such subjects as physics or chemistry in the tongue in which God spoke to Moses? A violent reaction took place. The three Zionist committee members, among them the writer and essayist Aḥad Ha-Am, resigned from the board. The teachers and pupils from all the schools of Palestine went on mass demonstrations and held their classes in the streets. The demonstrations spread even to many Jewish communities abroad. At the same time, a number of Hebrew linguists set themselves the task of supplying the missing technological words in the Hebrew vocabulary. Finally the Yekes (a derogatory though friendly name for the German Jews) retreated. So it was that Pythagoras, Pascal, and Marie Curie were taught in the language of Moses, King Solomon, and Isaiah.

Renewing the Holy Language in the Holy Land

In 1922 the British Mandate gave Hebrew official recognition as one of the three state languages, on a level with Arabic and English. For the first time since the sovereignty of Eretz Israel, Hebrew letters appeared on coins, as well as on stamps. Hebrew not only became the link with the past and the homogenizing medium of the various Jewish groups, it also helped new settlers to find a more intimate relationship with the somewhat fearsome landscape. The strange environment became more familiar when associated with biblical memories.

Hebrew became the symbol of the renaissance; the linguistic metamorphosis became a force, probably a dominant force, in the act of total transformation.

Lord Balfour at the opening ceremony of the Hebrew University, Jerusalem

The Central Zionist Archives, Jerusalem, Israel

The Central Zionist Archives, Jerusalem, Israel

The Central Zionist Archives, Jerusalem, Israel

First building of Hebrew University

Inauguration of Einstein Institute at the Hebrew University, Jerusalem

Albert Einstein and Menaḥem Mendel Ussishkin (a Zionist leader and delegate to the First Zionist Congress) in Jerusalem

The Central Zionist Archives, Jerusalem, Israel

XI

Theater and Art

The first amateur theatrical group, Ḥovevei ha-Bimah Ha-Ivri ("Lovers of the Hebrew Stage"): Jaffa, 1900

Theater Museum, Tel Aviv, Israel

THERE were rites and rituals in biblical Eretz Israel which were rich theatrical spectacles. But secular theater was always despised by the religious establishment. In ancient Israel the Roman occupying forces built imposing amphitheaters in Caesarea and Bet Shean that are standing to this day. The repertoire no doubt consisted of classical drama with the usual element of primitive revelry. The religious Jews led a vigorous campaign against that "house of mockery and fools," primarily because of the immoral and pagan content. Another reason was the threat of foreign influence upon the spiritual values of Judaism.

The fight against theater was continued in the later countries of exile. The only spectacles tolerated were the Purim plays performed in synagogue courtyards by local talent or wandering groups but even then looked upon with disdain. It often happened that such spectacles were banned and the texts of the plays destroyed. But in spite of this ban, many Jews participated as spectators or even actors and playwrights in the theater of European countries.

Toward the end of the nineteenth century, the Jewish theater (usually performed in Yiddish but occasionally in Hebrew) became an important cultural factor among the Jewish masses in eastern Europe and in America. Almost at the same time, there were attempts to produce plays in Palestine. There are records of amateur performances in Jerusalem and Jaffa as far back as 1905, when a group was formed in

Theater Museum, Tel Aviv, Israel

A traveling theatrical company, 1905

Jaffa, the first drama society in Palestine. The plays, brought over from eastern Europe, mostly historical plays by the "Father of the Jewish Theater," Abraham Goldfaden, were played in Yiddish, until the company one day decided to produce *Uriel Acosta*, by Karl Gutzkow. For the first time, the organizers insisted that the play be performed in Hebrew. The spectacle was so successful that it stimulated others to found a group, Ḥovevei ha-Bimah ha-Ivri (Lovers of the Hebrew Stage), and from then on Hebrew theater became not only an occasion for artistic experience but also an instrument for Hebrew education.

Theater and Art

Even in its primitive form, the theater played an important role in the process of re-establishing Hebrew as a living medium. The amateur groups had no scenery and no professional actors or directors. The compensation for this was the growing enthusiasm of the early audiences. The theater was mobile: a group of actors would arrive at a settlement in a horse-drawn wagon and play on an improvised stage made of wooden boxes or bundles of straw. If the theater was crude, it reflected the crudity of the surrounding life. But it contained the seeds that developed gradually into a more sophisticated and accomplished theater.

Amateur theatrical group, 1904

Theater Museum, Tel Aviv, Israel

Theater Museum, Tel Aviv, Israel

Theater group playing Tchibikoff's Jews, *1906*

Improvised stage on a kibbutz

The construction of a stage on a kibbutz

Theater Museum, Tel Aviv, Israel

Theater Museum, Tel Aviv, Israel

Theater Museum, Tel Aviv, Israel

Theater Museum, Tel Aviv, Israel

Theater Museum, Tel Aviv, Israel

Chaim Weizmann, the future President of Israel (seated third from left), among Ohel actors

Ohel, Israel's first workers' theater, founded in 1925 by the cultural committee of Histadrut

Sholem Aleichem's comedy Thrown to the Wind, 1919

Theater Museum, Tel Aviv, Israel

First satirical theater troop, Matateh ("Broom"). Founded in 1927.

Theater Museum, Tel Aviv, Israel

Members of Ha-Bimah ("The Stage"), a Hebrew theater company founded in Moscow in 1917, went to Palestine in 1928.

In 1921 a group was formed that called itself Teatron Ivri (Hebrew Theater), the first professional company. It started with many handicaps. The founders had to do without professional directors, stagehands, makeup artists—without whom a theater can hardly exist. There were no native plays; the repertoire consisted of imported plays by Strindberg, Ibsen, and Chekhov, and plays translated from Yiddish writers such as Sholem Aleichem, Peretz Hirschbein, and I. L. Peretz. The public, though by no means uncritical, was friendly and receptive, which encouraged the company to spread farther. They traveled from Tel Aviv to Haifa, to Jerusalem, to the settlements of Deganyah, Rosh Pinnah, Ḥaderah, Zikhron Yaakov, and to many other places. After a day of work in the fields, the audience would sit on planks or on the ground to enjoy the magic that flowed from the raised stage as they listened to *The Cherry Orchard* or *Tevye the Milkman.*

Theater was one of the areas of art that accompanied the physical efforts of building the *Yishuv*. At the turn of the century, a Jewish Lithuanian-born sculptor, Boris Schatz, mentioned to Theodor Herzl a plan to found a school for the arts in Palestine. Herzl was quite receptive to the idea, and the plan was formally approved and developed, in 1905, by the Seventh Zionist Congress. A year later, Boris Schatz settled in Jerusalem, where, along with a few other artists, he opened a school of arts and crafts, which they named Bezalel, after the architect of the biblical Tabernacle, who was also an engraver and a designer of the priests' garments. The establishment of such a school broke new ground despite the small population, the paucity of support, and the hostility of the orthodox Jews, who considered all kinds of plastic art, and particularly sculpture, a sin against the second commandment: "Thou shalt not make unto thee any graven image."

But the school attracted many other artists and students. Even artists from abroad came, dazzled by the colorfulness of the land, its brilliant light, and the exoticism of the oriental Jews and the Muslims. Here they thought to fulfill an old dream, of creating a national Jewish style in art.

Like the pioneers who came determined to revive the dead and arid land, the artists, too, came with a mission to revive the symbolism and sacredness of the Bible and to keep alive the spirit of the Jewish legends and folklore. Their aim was to create a thoroughly Jewish style. They hoped to achieve this by turning their backs on the traumatic experiences of exile and devote their art to the new, exotic landscape of Palestine.

Among the first who laid the foundations of this art in painting and in sculpture were Boris Schatz, Abel Pann, Ephraim Lilien, Naḥum Gutman, Israel Paldi, and Reuven Rubin. Their insistence on creating a new style of art, free of European culture, was not easy to fulfill. Each of them, almost without exception, came from eastern Europe and brought along the artistic traditions of his place of birth. Many of them had finally to compromise and use the European technique to illustrate the Jewish tradition, with the emphasis not so much on the pictorial as on the decorative. In 1920 an organization of Jewish artists was formed, and three years later the first public exhibition, in the Tower of David, took place, within the walls of Old Jerusalem.

The Central Zionist Archives, Jerusalem, Israel

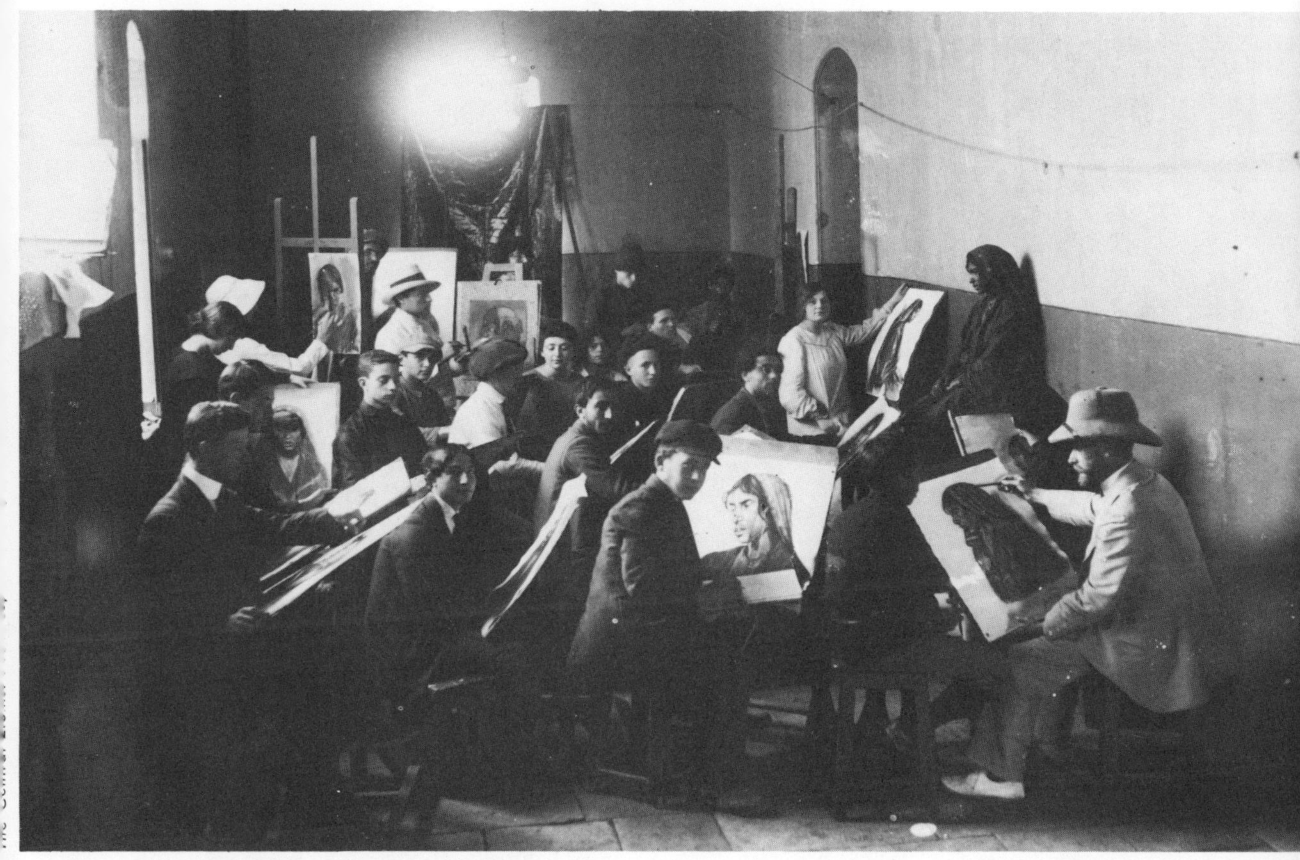

Bezalel classroom: Jerusalem, 1910

The opening of a Bezalel exhibition in Lvov, Poland, 1909. Seated third from left is Boris Schatz, founder of Bezalel Art School, in Palestine.

The Central Zionist Archives, Jerusalem, Israel

The Zionist Archives and Library, New York

The Central Zionist Archives, Jerusalem, Israel

Bezalel students honor Herzl, 1912

Bezalel Art School under the Turks: Jerusalem, 1910

Silversmith at the Bezalel school, 1912

First orchestra: Rishon le-Zion, 1900

Another branch of art began to emerge, that of music. It began with songs, which the *olim* had brought along from their homes. From the very beginning, the settlements rang with a strange combination of Ukrainian, Polish, and Romanian tunes, the old lyrics being replaced by Hebrew words. The result was not a misalliance, as one might expect, but a perfectly harmonious marriage. The background of the desolate, lonely, and mystical landscape chimed well with the languishing tunes of Russian ballads and Ukrainian love songs. Some of the pioneers had brought along garmoshkas, balalaikas, and mandolins, to which were added oriental *halilim*, stringed instruments, and drums. Almost all the developing settlements had choirs; soon some towns began to form small brass bands for occasions of public celebration.

Theater and Art

In chronicles of life in the early settlements it is invariably mentioned that after a strenuous day in the fields there were dancing and communal singing. One of the diarists of the *biluim* wrote, "This wasn't just an expression of joy or a demonstration of comradeship; it also was needed as an expression of self-assurance that what 'we are doing is right.' "

Soon there was a need to establish schools for those who desired to study instrument playing or singing. The first music school was founded in Tel Aviv in 1910; it attracted seventy-five pupils in the first year. Another school, Bet Leviyyim, was founded in 1914. Jerusalem had its first music school in 1918, and Haifa in 1928.

Performing in the streets of Rishon le-Zion

The Central Zionist Archives, Jerusalem, Israel

In 1923 Mordechai Galinski arrived in Palestine and organized the first opera company. In 1924 regular concerts were given in Jerusalem. In 1925 Joel Engel organized regular concerts in Tel Aviv. In the same year, the *Yishuv* had its first choir festival. Ballet schools were established as early as 1920. Many immigrants brought over dances from their countries of origin: the *hora* from Romania, Ḥasidic dances from eastern Europe, and the *debka* from Arab countries. In 1920 a ballet school established by Rina Nikova began to develop a biblical ballet utilizing Yemenite traditions.

XII

Holidays

Passover Seder for Jewish troops: Jerusalem, 1919

The Central Zionist Archives, Jerusalem, Israel

Most Jewish holidays originated in biblical times and had a dual origin: historical and agricultural. In the course of the almost two thousand years of exile, the agricultural character had dimmed and become irrelevant, its significance being largely misunderstood. For instance the holiday of *Passover*, which is celebrated in remembrance of the exodus from Egypt and as the festival of national redemption, had also the agricultural import of being the festival of spring, of the paschal sacrifice, the offering of the first fruits—either of a lamb (Ḥag ha-Peṣaḥ) or of the earliest grain (Hag ha-Matzot).

Similarly the holiday of *Sukkot* historically celebrates the journey of the children of Israel through the desert after the exodus from Egypt, during which they lived in booths (*sukkot*) of a temporary nature. The holiday is therefore celebrated with the construction of *sukkot*. Agriculturally the holiday represents the final gathering of the fruit and the products of the year. That aspect is referred to as Ḥag ha-Asiph, the holiday of ingathering. Both *Passover* and *Sukkot* were occasions when the inhabitants of ancient Eretz Israel made pilgrimages to Jerusalem.

A third pilgrim festival was *Shavuot*, called Yom ha-Katzir, (the Day of Harvest). Again, its other aspect was historical. It celebrated the time of receiving the Torah, in commemoration of the six hundred thousand Jews who left Egypt and stood gathered at the foot of the mountain of Sinai hearing God's voice.

Food-gathering in Rishon le-Zion

The Central Zionist Archives, Jerusalem, Israel

Bringing a torah to shul: *Jerusalem, 1920*

The Central Zionist Archives, Jerusalem, Israel

The graves of the Maccabees: Ḥanukkah, 1909

In the countries of dispersion all those three major holidays were celebrated for their historical rather than their agricultural significance. The same applies to *Rosh Ha-Shana,* which with *Yom Kippur* is a day of emotional introspection and atonement. But *Rosh Ha-Shana* in ancient Eretz Israel was the beginning of the New Year, marking the birthday of the world, the joyous remembrance of creation.

Even the holiday of *Ḥanukkah,* which commemorates the national revolt of the Maccabees against the occupying powers of the Hellenistic Syrians and the miracle with the little cruse of oil that burned for eight days in the Temple, has a second meaning. In biblical times it was a winter festival, which celebrated the lengthening daylight and the kindling of fire at the dedication of the Temple's altar. In both meanings the central motif is light.

Holidays

A purely agricultural holiday is the *Rosh Ha-Shana le-Ilanot* (the New Year for Trees), which marks the date from which to count the age of a tree. In the Diaspora this was a day when it was customary to eat Israeli fruit, mostly carob or boxer. *Purim*, on the other hand, is a purely historical holiday. It commemorates in a joyous and carnival spirit the defeat of an archenemy of the Jewish people, Haman, and the triumph of the Jews thanks to the wisdom of Mordecai and the charms of his young niece, Esther, whom he had cleverly married to King Ahasuerus.

Purim carnival: Tel Aviv, 1928

The Central Zionist Archives, Jerusalem, Israel

The Jewish Daily Forward, New York

This little girl was voted "Queen of the Trees" at the New Year's Festival for Trees

The Central Zionist Archives, Jerusalem, Israel

Children dressing up for Purim: Tel Aviv

With the return to the Promised Land, the agricultural aspect of the holidays regained its relevance. The holidays of winter, spring, and summer again chimed with the calendar and the local climatic conditions; and such holiday prayers as that for rain and dew ceased to be only a reminder of the past. To the pioneers of the new agricultural settlements, the prayers recaptured their original significance.

One of the minor holidays, *Lag Ba-Omer*, was a holiday for children in the countries of dispersion, who on that day went out into the country armed with bows and arrows. In Israel, *Lag Ba-Omer* is a folk festival. *Lag Ba-Omer* means the thirty-third day between *Passover* (the Day of Deliverance) and *Shavuot* (the Day of the Encounter with

God). According to the Bible, it is a *mitzvah* to count the forty-nine days in a special manner, being the time of the approach to Mount Zion and the revelation of God. The entire period is a time of semimourning, when no weddings are allowed. Even hair cutting is forbidden, because of a plague that killed many of the students of Rabbi Akiva, at Bene Berak, at the time of Bar Kokhba. On the thirty-third day, the plague stopped, so on that day all the bans are lifted. This is why this thirty-third day of Omer (*Lag Ba-Omer*) was a holiday for school children in the shtetl. In Israel, people visit the grave of one of the rabbis who died in the plague, the author of the mystical *Zohar*, Reb Simeon ben Yoḥai. He was buried on Mount Meron, near Safed, and the custom of visiting his grave became a folk holiday. When the new settlers came to Palestine, they began to join the Old *Yishuv* in its yearly pilgrimage to the grave and to dance at night around bonfires all over the land.

A Lag Ba-Omer festival in Meron, an ancient village in Upper Galilee, where Rabbi Simeon ben Yoḥai was buried, about eighteen hundred years ago. Lag Ba-Omer: Meron, 1912

The Central Zionist Archives, Jerusalem, Israel

The Central Zionist Archives, Jerusalem, Israel

Lag Ba-Omer: Meron, 1912

In the revived land, all festivals have acquired a public character. On the Sabbath, work is stopped, shops and offices shut down, and public transportation is suspended. No amusement places remain open on the evening of *Tishah B'Av*, the anniversary of the destruction of the Temple. *Purim* has become a popular carnival, with thousands of children dressed in bright costumes and disguised as the characters of the *Megillah* (the Book of Esther) parading in the streets of the villages and towns. During the holiday of *Ḥanukkah*, great eight-branched candelabra are lit in front of public buildings and in the open squares of

La Ba-Omer: Meron, 1921

every *kibbutz* and *moshav*. During the three pilgrim festivals, thousands of new immigrants renew the ancient custom of "ascending" to Jerusalem. In agricultural settlements have emerged new patterns of festival observance. In the secular *kibbutzim* the religious aspects are given a lay interpretation. The reaping of the Omer is celebrated on the second day of *Passover*. The bringing of *bikkurim* (first fruits) is observed on the night of *Shavuot*. The night of the Seder, both in religious and nonreligious settlements, is transformed into a large public festival.

All the Jewish festivals that in the countries of exile were simply family holidays have in the new land become festivals of a revived nation.

XIII
Epilogue

The biluim . . . *years later*

The Zionist Archives and Library, New York

THE majority of the photos in this book belong to the period of the first three *Aliyot*. With few exceptions they all depict the period of the thirty-two years between the landing of the first group of *biluim*, at the port of Jaffa, and the outbreak of the First World War, when emigration stopped.

Thirty-two years is a brief episode in human history, but Jewish history operates in different dimensions. In relation to the almost two thousand years of exile, these thirty-two years were filled with unprecedented drama. Not in terms of real accomplishments, for all the three *Aliyot* had done was to bring into Palestine a population of fewer than ninety thousand scattered through a few dozen settlements and towns. But their significance cannot be measured in statistics.

For the thousands of young men and women who had set out on their Way of Ascension, this was a most unusual time. It was a time when each of them believed that he was part of a historical wave and was being swept along by a phenomenon called "purpose." It was a time when metaphors were no longer figures of speech but were taken in their most literal sense; when "struggle for existence" meant just that: a struggle for physical survival. When "sacrificing oneself" meant a sacrifice with the possibility of personal death.

It was a time when every second of the present was believed to hold a seed of the future, and when the future was believed to be an extension of the present, with all its rich idealism undiminished.

The thousands of human faces shown in this book, the individual portraits and the collective groups, represent the fulfillment of the prophesied "ingathering of the people." But what a bizarre ingathering it was!

We possess no photographs or sketches of the Jewish men and women who lived in biblical times, but in all probability the Jews who were expelled from their land two thousand years ago were, for the most part, if not identical with at least similar to the men and women depicted in the contemporary statues and drawings preserved in the museums of Cairo and London and the monuments of Persepolis.

Now, two millenniums later, the Jews of the kingdom of Judah have come back so transformed that had one of their ancestors been on hand to welcome them, he would have had the shock of his life. The many countries of dispersion wrought strange changes in their physical appearance. We assume that their ancestors were a homogenous Middle-Eastern group, but the descendants now came back in all shapes and colors, a spectrum of pigmentation, diverse shades of skin, hair, and eyes; some even resemble Ukrainian, White Russian, or Polish peasants.

The only biblical woman whose features are described in detail, the black-eyed and black-haired Shulamith, of the Song of Songs, would be startled to see how her granddaughters now came back as blue-eyed Yekaterinas, milk-skinned Jadwigas, or straw-haired Marias. The ingathered people returned like a miniature assembly of the whole of humanity.

But even more than in their physical appearance were the differences in their culture, in the diversified forms of behavior, gestures, speech, and laughter; in their newly acquired standards of living, ways of dressing, and tastes in food. Even their belief in the one and unifying Jehovah had picked up, on the long way, elements of alien beliefs and mythologies.

But what united them and more than outweighed these vast differences was awareness that they had all come back to a place that had once been their common point of departure, that the historical circle had closed.

Of all the photos in this book, the most picturesque and colorful are undoubtedly those of the Orientals—such as the Yemenites, who are little men, their faces invariably framed in curly beards and *peyot*, their women often startlingly beautiful, with the most delicate features and large, liquid eyes; and the other exotic Jewish types from Bokhara, Iraq, Tunisia, and Afghanistan. They seem to belong in Palestine, to be an organic part of the landscape.

The Jewish Daily Forward, New York

Aged Jews studying holy books in the Holy Land, 1922

The Jewish Daily Forward, New York

Children of pioneers in Kibbutz Ein Harod, 1923

But, for dramatic content, it is the others, those with less spectacular costumes and faces—the boys and girls from eastern Europe—who will be remembered for the part they played in this most fateful episode of Jewish history; those most romantic of lovers, the Lovers of Zion, the *ḥalutzim* in the *hakhsharas*, preparing themselves with devotion for the tasks of the new land. These same young men and women, after wanderings often more painful than the forty years of legendary wanderings in the desert, finally arrived, and we see them now living in tents among dunes and rocks, draining swamps, plowing a tough, malevolent, stubborn earth, building the first shed, planting the very first tree, and believing that with each blade of grass they brought forth from a soil that had for centuries lain fallow, they were performing an act of divine resurrection.

It was to them that Herzl had said, "If you will it—it will not be a legend." They willed it, and built what they believed to be the legend.

Appendixes

Table of Historical Events in European Jewry

Mid-nineteenth century Enlightment period characterized by a pronounced tendency to assimilation.

1862 Moses Hess, a former collaborator of Marx and Engels, published *Rome and Jerusalem,* a book advocating national liberation for the Jews by the creation of a Jewish state.

1881 Pogrom in Warsaw.

1882 The first modern Zionist pioneering group, composed of fourteen young Jews (called *biluim*), from Kharkov, Russia, set out for Palestine to transform a two-thousand-year-old dream into a reality.

1882 A group of Russian Jews formed the movement Hibbat Zion ("Love of Zion") as a result of the 1881 pogroms.

1892 Theodor Herzl published his utopian novel *Altneuland* ("The Renewed Old Land").

1894 A furious wave of anti-Semitism swept over France as a consequence of the trial of Alfred Dreyfus, a French Jewish army officer accused of treason.

1896 Publication of Theodor Herzl's *Judenstaat.*

1897 The First Zionist Congress was held in Basel.

1915 A pioneering youth movement formed a federation called He-Ḥalutz ("The Pioneer"), which concerned itself with the agricultural and pioneer training of Jewish youth, and their immigration to Israel.

1933 Adolf Hitler attains power in Germany.

1935 Nuremberg Laws.

Table of Jewish Historical Events in Palestine

1882 The first collective settlement, Rishon le-Zion ("The First in Zion"), was founded by the *biluim.*

1897 Teḥiyyat Israel ("Revival of Israel") was created by a group of people devoted to reviving the Hebrew language.

1901 The Jewish National Fund, an organization devoted to buying, developing, and cultivating the land in Palestine as national property, was set up by the World Zionist Organization.

1905 At the Seventh Zionist Congress, for the first time, the Arab question was officially recognized.

1908 The building of the first communal agricultural settlement, Deganyah ("Cornflower").

1909 Dedication ceremony for the founding of Tel Aviv.

1917 The British Government issued the Balfour Declaration, which promised that Jews would be allowed to establish their own homeland.

1920 The founding of Histadrut, the Israel trade-union federation.

1921 The first threat of "an all-out war" between the Jews and Arabs.

1921 Tel Aviv ceased to be a suburb of Jaffa and acquired the status of a municipality.

1922 A British mandate recognized Hebrew as one of the three state languages (with Arabic and English).

1925 Official ceremony for the founding of Hebrew University.

Table of Historical Events in American Jewry

–By 1880 The Jewish population had increased to some 250,000, mainly of German origin.

–After the pogroms of 1881, great numbers of Russian refugees arrived, changing the entire flavor of American Jewry.

–1892 American Jewish Historical Society founded to promote the study of American Jewish history.

1892 Founding of the *Forward,* New York's Yiddish daily newspaper. It began as the organ of the Jewish labor movement and of the Jewish socialists.

1906 American Jewish Committee founded to protect the civil, religious, economic, social, and educational rights of Jews in all parts of the world.

1914 American Jewish Joint Distribution Committee created as American Jewry's overseas relief and rehabilitation agency.

1914 American Zion Commonwealth, a land-purchasing agency, dedicates itself to the redemption of land in Palestine and developing Jewish settlement there.

1917 American Jewish Congress founded for the purpose of securing the recognition of Jewish civil, political, and religious equal rights in central and eastern Europe, as well as to protect Jewish rights in Palestine.

1919–20 American Academy for Jewish Research created to promote Jewish learning and research in America (incorporated in 1929).

1939 American Association for Jewish Education founded to provide services in the fields of educational research and community organization for Jewish education, personnel training, and welfare.

PALESTINE
1925
MILES
0
20
KM
0
20
N
E
S
W
MEDITERRANEAN

LITANY R.
Tyre
LEBANON
Tel Hai
LAKE HULEH
SYRIA
Kibbutz Ayelet Hashachar
Meron
Safed
Rosh Pinnah
JORDAN R.
Acre
GALILEE
SEA OF GALILEE (SEA OF KINNERET)
Haifa
Tiberias
Kibbutz Yagur
Kibbutz Kinneret
KIBBUTZ DEGANYAH
Nazareth
YARMUK R.
VALLEY OF JEZREEL
Afula
KIBBUTZ MERHAVYAH
Zichron Yakov
Megiddo
Kibbutz Ein Harod
Bet Alpha
Caesarea
Bet Shean
Jenin
Haderah
Nablus
RIVER
JORDAN